METAETHICS, EGOISM, AND VIRTUE

The Ayn Rand Society (www.aynrandsociety.org), founded in 1987 and affiliated from its inception with the American Philosophical Association, Eastern Division, has as its constitutional purpose "to foster the study by philosophers of the philosophical thought and writings of Ayn Rand." Since 1988, the society has sponsored some twenty programs at Eastern Division meetings and in 2008 it began sponsoring programs at Pacific Division meetings, as well.

In furtherance of its purpose, the society is publishing, with the University of Pittsburgh Press, a series of volumes called Ayn Rand Society Philosophical Studies. Each volume will be unified around a theme of importance both to philosophy generally and to Rand's philosophical system, Objectivism, in particular, and will be intended to be of interest both to philosophers unfamiliar with Rand and to specialists in her thought. The volumes will contain, for the most part, previously unpublished materials that pertain to Rand's philosophical work; the aim is to present professional studies that will advance understanding both of the philosophical issues involved and of the thought of this seminal and still underappreciated philosopher.

Ayn Rand Society Philosophical Studies

Allan Gotthelf, Editor

James G. Lennox, Associate Editor

METAETHICS, EGOISM, AND VIRTUE

Studies in Ayn Rand's Normative Theory

Allan Gotthelf, Editor

James G. Lennox, Associate Editor

AYN RAND SOCIETY PHILOSOPHICAL STUDIES

University of Pittsburgh Press

Published by the University of Pittsburgh Press, Pittsburgh, Pa., 15260
Copyright © 2011, University of Pittsburgh Press
Manufactured in the United States of America
Printed on acid-free paper
10 9 8 7 6 5 4 3 2 1

Library of Congress Cataloging-in-Publication Data

Metaethics, egoism, and virtue : studies in Ayn Rand's normative theory / Allan Gotthelf,
editor ; James G. Lennox, associate editor.
     p.   cm. — (Ayn Rand Society philosophical studies)
 Includes bibliographical references and index.
 ISBN 978-0-8229-4400-3 (cloth : alk. paper)
 1. Rand, Ayn. 2. Normativity (Ethics) 3. Egoism. 4. Virtue. I. Gotthelf, Allan, 1942–
II. Lennox, James G.
 B945.R234M47 2011
 191—dc22   2010031521

CONTENTS

Though Ayn Rand is still best known among philosophers for her support of egoism in ethics and capitalism in politics, there is increasingly widespread awareness of both the range and the systematic character of her thought. The present volume, *Metaethics, Egoism, and Virtue: Studies in Ayn Rand's Normative Theory*, focuses not on the metaphysical and epistemological fundamentals of Rand's thought, but on aspects of her ethical theory. Though Rand's endorsement of ethical egoism is well known—one of her most familiar essay collections is *The Virtue of Selfishness (VOS)*—the character of her egoism is less well known, and its validation even less so. Those who know the title of *VOS* often don't remember its subtitle, *A New Concept of Egoism*, or give sufficient significance in reading it to the term "new." Scholars are increasingly coming to understand Rand's normative ethics as virtue-based (in no small part due to Tara Smith's recent book, *Ayn Rand's Normative Ethics: The Virtuous Egoist*). Yet philosophers are still not sufficiently familiar with the objective theory of value and the moral psychology (and, more broadly, the view of human nature) that ground the way in which Rand's ethical theory is (and isn't) virtue-based as well as the particular traits it endorses as virtues.

Like any fundamentally teleological ethics, Rand's faces the challenge of accounting for the status of the value that it identifies as our ultimate end: What makes this value an ultimate end for us, and how can it be established to be so? In our leadoff chapter, Darryl Wright explores how Rand's distinctive view of the role of reason in conceiving and committing to ends provides her with a strikingly original response to this challenge. Among the issues Wright addresses is whether, and in what way, moral obligation depends for Rand on a premoral "choice to live." This has been a matter of controversy among philosophers interested in Rand. Douglas Rasmussen has argued that the applicability of moral norms does not for Rand depend on such a choice, while Allan Gotthelf has argued that it does. That discussion is represented in the first section of this volume.

The second section features an engaging and illuminating exchange between Irfan Khawaja and Paul Bloomfield on the relationship between Rand's Objectivism and analytic philosophy.

In the volume's third section, Christine Swanton, best known for her work on virtue ethics, holds that there is, in both Nietzsche and Rand, a virtuous form of egoism, and that some forms of altruism are indeed vicious, but argues that one must also recognize, even on Rand's premises, that there is a virtuous form of altruism. Her discussion is followed by Darryl Wright's spirited and very helpful comments.

Tara Smith's *Ayn Rand's Normative Ethics: The Virtuous Egoist*, mentioned above, is the subject of the final section of the volume. Helen Cullyer, Christine Swanton, and Lester Hunt all comment upon Smith's work, and Smith responds to each in turn.

This volume has been a pleasure to put together, not least because of the unfailing cooperation of our contributors, and the advice and assistance of our editorial board. The inauguration of the series at this time is due in significant part to the urging of Gregory Salmieri, who convinced us that the time was right, and to the 2009 Ayn Rand Society steering committee, which made the actual decision to begin the series. We are grateful to one of our contributors, Irfan Khawaja, for suggesting the title for this volume, to Deborah Meade for her care and judgment in editorial matters, and to Ben Bayer for his astute indexing. Most of all, we are indebted to Cynthia Miller, director of the University of Pittsburgh Press, for her support, her vision, and her wise advice.

Neither the editors nor the editorial board necessarily endorse the content of work published in the series, and we may on occasion publish writings one or more of us think "gets it all wrong," so long as these writings are respectful of Rand and her work and further the aims of the series. We intend to publish only professional work of a quality that seriously engages topics of importance both philosophically in general and in Rand's thought in particular.

It is with great pleasure, then, that we present the first book in this series, a collection of essays aimed at illuminating central aspects of Ayn Rand's distinctive ethical theory.

REASON, CHOICE, AND THE ULTIMATE END

Reasoning about Ends
Life as a Value in Ayn Rand's Ethics
DARRYL WRIGHT

> I reject the evil idea that choosing ends by reason
> is impossible. It has destroyed ethics. Everything
> that I have written is devoted to proving the
> opposite.
> —AYN RAND, 1969

In Ayn Rand's view, ethics has a teleological foundation. There is an end that serves as the standard for defining moral values and virtues, and in relation to this end, moral norms impose obligations. The reason-giving force of these obligations, all things considered, depends on what normative status Rand accords the end that morality serves. And on this she is unambiguous. The end for which morality is needed is also the ultimate end for a rational agent qua rational agent and the foundation of all of such an agent's (normative) reasons for action. These reasons, in Rand's view, are always of a fundamentally teleological sort, that is, they are reasons to do or seek something as a means to something else.[1]

Much of the work on this article was done during a semester spent as a visiting scholar at the Social Philosophy and Policy Center in the spring of 2007. I'm grateful to the center and its staff for providing a wonderful environment in which to pursue and discuss my work on this and other projects.

Epigraph: This was part of Rand's answer to a question about her ethical theory after a 1969 lecture at the Ford Hall Forum. See *Q&A* 107.

1. The means may in some cases be a constitutive rather than an instrumental means, that is, a type of activity that is an instance of some more abstract type (as running is an instance of exercising) or that is a part of some more complex activity (as working is a part of living one's life).

Thus, in Rand's view, everyone who has (normative) reasons for acting has reasons for being moral. Further, she argues that the relationship between morality and its telos is such that those reasons are indefeasible; there are no other reasons capable of trumping them.

I outline Rand's ethical thought with emphasis on the sort of justification she offers for an ultimate rational end, and the relation between this end and the requirements of morality. Already we can see a kind of puzzle or paradox that her view may seem to confront: if all reasons for action are teleological, how can anything be a rational ultimate end? For we cannot give a teleological reason for making something an ultimate end, yet if something is a rational end, must not an agent have a reason to hold it?

Standard Approaches to the Rationality of Ends

I want to consider four well-known views about the rationality of ultimate ends from which Rand's view can be distinguished. Historically, these views are associated with Hume, Moore, Kant, and Aristotle, respectively. Since these views have heavily influenced contemporary discussions of practical rationality, we can gain a sense of where Rand's views stand in relation to currently debated positions. By highlighting the ways in which Rand's position diverges from standard theories about the rationality of ends and bringing these divergences out, we can frame a problem for which her own theory proposes a solution.

When Rand refers to "the evil idea that choosing ends by reason is impossible," probably foremost in her mind is the view that Hume defends in book 2 of the *Treatise of Human Nature* and in the *Enquiry Concerning the Principles of Morals*. According to Hume, our ends are determined by our passions, and an end of mine can be contrary to reason only if the passion that gives me this end is so. But a passion, Hume says, can be contrary to reason only "when founded on a false supposition, or when it chooses means insufficient for" an end we already have in our sights (*Treatise* 2.3.3.6). By definition, the passions responsible for our ultimate ends never have the second kind of defect, since we seek ultimate ends for their own sake. Our passions can, however, have the first kind of defect, being caused by false beliefs about that to which the passion attaches us. For example, a person's passion for his ultimate end of knowing God could be caused partly by the "false supposition" that God exists. The passion would to that extent be unreasonable, according to Hume. But it is only in this minimal sense that a passion for an end could be rationally defective. Our beliefs about what exists fix the possible scope of our most basic desires, and thus can affect what desires we come to have, but these desires themselves are "original existences" and reflect neither adherence to reason nor resistance to reason. Thus, Hume notoriously says, "'[t]is not contrary to reason for me to choose my total ruin, to prevent the least uneasiness of an Indian or person wholly unknown to me. 'Tis as little contrary to reason to prefer even my own acknowledg'd lesser good to my greater, and have a more ardent affection for the former than the latter" (*Treatise* 2.3.3.6). These preferences might simply reflect the relative strength of our passions for these different ends.

For Humean views[2] of practical rationality to be plausible, the passions attaching us to our ultimate values must be nonrational desires (or else they would be rationally evaluable). It is clear that Rand does not hold this kind of view of desire. Her own view of desire is suggested, for instance, in the following passage discussing the concept of a person's "interests": "A man's 'interests' depend on the kind of goals he chooses to pursue, his choice of goals depends on his desires, his desires depend on his values—and, for a rational man, his values depend on the judgment of his mind" (*VOS* 57). She adds that a rational person "does not act to achieve a desire until and unless he is able rationally to validate it *in the full context of his knowledge* and of his other values and goals. He does not act until he is able to say: 'I want it because it is *right*'" (*VOS* 58). Rand here characterizes desires as having an underlying evaluative basis: we desire what we value, and the normative judgments underlying our values can be rational or irrational. The rationality or irrationality of our values ramifies up through the chain to the desires, goals, and interests that are founded on them. It will be rational (or irrational) to desire something as an end insofar as it is rational (or irrational) to value it as an end. The problem with Humean views, from Rand's perspective, is that they mistakenly treat our desires for our ends as primaries—as basic psychological

---

2. Since the purpose of this discussion is to explore what kind of rational warrant attaches to ends, I have only specified Hume's view (and the category "Humean views") as it concerns that issue. Thus, I have not commented directly on Hume's views about the rational warrant possessed by the (known and available) means to an accepted end. Specifically, I have not addressed whether Hume subscribes to some form of instrumental norm, on which reason directs us to do that which will most effectively realize our ends. Interpretations of Hume's view differ on this point, as do assessments of contemporary Hume-inspired views that feature such a norm but deny reason a role in prescribing ends. But Rand would reject any view that treated desires for ends as nonrational responses and that, on this basis, followed Hume in denying reason such a role.

phenomena ("original existences")—and thus erroneously conclude that desires are subjective responses immune to rational criticism.

The view that goals and desires depend on values, which (when rational) depend on rational judgment, opens up the question of what makes a judgment of value rational, and, since our concern here lies especially with the rationality of ends, what makes it rational to value something as an end. One influential answer to this question is that it is rational to value something as an end insofar as it is intrinsically such as to be valued, meaning that it has some particular form of intrinsic value that warrants our valuing it and acknowledging its value in our actions. Intrinsic value theories, in the sense I mean, compose a wide class. They can be metaphysically realist, positing that intrinsic values exist or subsist independently of our thinking about them.[3] But an intrinsic value theory need not be developed as a form of value realism; in a Kantian spirit, it might instead take the form of a theory of practical reasoning in which a commitment to certain intrinsic values is held to be a constitutive feature of rational agency. Kant, for instance, took it to be constitutive of rational agency to act only on maxims expressing respect for humanity as an end in itself (*Groundwork,* Ak. 427–31 [Kant 1998]). Another axis of variation among these theories concerns the putative bearers of value, which might for instance be persons, actions, maxims, states of affairs, or natural or artificial objects such as mountains or artworks. What these theories have in common is the ascription—either as a realist claim or as a practical presupposition—of a form of normative value that grounds desire-independent reasons to act on behalf of whatever bears this value.[4] For instance, if malnutrition and the suffering it causes are intrinsically bad, and proper nourishment for people is intrinsically good, then everyone has some (not necessarily conclusive) reason to divert resources to the relief of malnutrition, whatever their desires and whatever their personal connection to those affected.

Rand criticizes intrinsic value theories for "divorc[ing] the concept of 'good' from beneficiaries, and the concept of 'value' from valuer and purpose—claiming that the good is good in, by, and of itself" (*CUI* 13).

---

3. G. E. Moore's writings are the locus classicus of this type of view, of course. See Moore 1993, chap. 1 and 280–98.

4. Different theories have different accounts of what "acting on behalf" of the value-bearers entails. For Moore (1993, chap. 5), to act on behalf of the good is to promote it, as for instance by producing it or protecting it. For Kant (*Groundwork,* Ak. 35–38 [1998]), to act on behalf of the value of rational nature is to respect it.

If something is intrinsically valuable, its realization or protection is supposed to be normative for one's actions whether or not one benefits in any way from that thing. Similarly, intrinsic values are supposed to be normative for one's action independently of whether they serve one's antecedently established purposes, and their value (qua intrinsic) is supposed to be independent of their *being valued*. Whereas Rand faults Humean theories for neglecting the evaluative basis of desires, she faults intrinsic value theories for neglecting the teleological basis of values, that is, their basis in the goals and purposes of living organisms: "'good' and 'value' pertain *only* to a living organism—to an individual living organism" (*CUI* 12). Related to this, she faults these theories for neglecting the connection between goods and benefits. The good of an organism is, from one perspective, that which benefits it. From another perspective, it is that which the organism values, "acts to gain and/or keep," in Rand's words (*VOS* 16).[5] Normative questions open up in a special way for humans because of the distinctive way in which these two aspects of value can come apart, as they do when what we value does *not* benefit us. Therein arises the need for evaluative standards and, Rand holds, the possibility of rational assessment of ends as well as means.

Rand sees the needs and goals of living organisms as providing a reference point for objective value judgments whose subject matter is what is good for a given organism or kind of organism. By contrast, intrinsic value theories confront a problem about objectivity, in her view. Judgments of intrinsic value are supposed to have a certain kind of objectivity, in virtue of which they can claim to provide a suitable basis for claims about how we have reason to act. But part of objectivity is intelligibility, and on intrinsic value views either the *value* of values is unintelligible to us (in the case of metaphysically realist views) or we are unintelligible to ourselves (in the case of Kantian views) (see *CUI* 13–15; *PWNI* 129–31). All we can say to make sense of our ascriptions of intrinsic value is that this is how the normative landscape strikes us (for realism) or that this is how we are constituted to value (for Kantianism). Rand thus sees the objectivity secured by these theories as being illusory, a mere claim of objectivity for what remain subjective value-responses (see *CUI* 15). This would be a controversial interpretation of the theories in question, of course, defensible only in the context of a developed account of objectivity. But my

---

5. Rand applies the generic sense of the term to the action of all living organisms; values, in this sense, are not necessarily purposively pursued.

interest here simply is in explaining why Rand sees the need to base her account of the role of reason in judging ends on a different kind of value theory.

Rand seeks a form of justification that allows for the rational assessment of ends without appealing to a form of intrinsic value. This philosophical project raises its own issue of objectivity, as is clear from some of the comments she makes about Kant's ethics. Kant argues that in acting for any of his ends, a rational agent must presuppose his own intrinsic worth qua rational. The intrinsic worth of rational nature, Kant argues, gives rise to the categorical imperative to impartially respect and promote the interests of all rational beings as ends in themselves. Contemporary neo-Kantians argue in a broadly similar vein for practical principles of respect for persons, principles that they maintain are reason-giving for every rational agent independently of his specific ends. But Rand excludes such intrinsically normative principles from her view of reasons for action:

> Reality confronts man with a great many "musts," but all of them are conditional; the formula of realistic necessity is: "You must, if—" (and the "if" stands for man's choice): "—if you want to achieve a certain goal. You must eat, if you want to survive. You must work, if you want to eat. You must think, if you want to work. You must look at reality, if you want to think—if you want to know what to do—if you want to know what goals to choose—if you want to know how to achieve them." (*PWNI* 133)

Rand holds that practical necessities, such as those mentioned in the above examples, are the foundation of reasons for action (and moral obligations to act). Broadly, we have reason to do that which it is necessary to do in order to achieve our (rational) ends. Thus principles of action derive their normativity from the end on which they are founded and that their implementation would serve. This point returns us to the issue of the rationality of ends. If all "oughts" are hypothetical, then there cannot be an "ought" directing us to our ultimate ends, the ends we (properly) seek for their own sake and not for the sake of anything further. Nor, for Rand, can these ends be ones we simply desire for their own sakes. As the previously quoted passage indicates, she views these ends as being chosen; but if the choices that attach us to our ultimate ends are arbitrary or unaccountable, Rand's account of practical reasoning will fail on its own terms. In order for Rand's view to achieve its aims, the choice of a (certain) ultimate end thus must be one for which, in some sense, there are rational grounds.

In exploring Rand's views in this area, it seems natural to seek connections to Aristotle, since Rand's overall philosophy is Aristotelian in a number of significant ways (see *VOR* chap. 2). But she says little about Aristotle's ethics, and what she says about the foundations of his ethics is quite critical. So I want to look briefly at why that might be.

Rand says that Aristotle "based his ethical system on observations of what the noble and wise men of his time chose to do, leaving unanswered the questions of: *why* they chose to do it and *why* he evaluated them as noble and wise" (*VOS* 14). This criticism focuses (I take it) on Aristotle's view that the judgment of the *phronimos*, the man of practical wisdom, is the proper standard of virtue. Though I do not have the space here to defend my interpretation of the objection, the problem Rand is focusing on seems to be, first, that by not considering why the *phronimos* acts, Aristotle leaves us without well-defined principles of action, and we may thus find ourselves unable reliably to extend his example to our own choices; this seems implied also in Rand's earlier point (clearly intended as criticism) that Aristotle does not regard ethics as an exact science (*VOS* 14). Perhaps the problem is also that we will lack justification for making the *phronimos* our model if we do not understand why he acts as he does. The second problem—concerning the basis of Aristotle's own evaluations— also seems to be one of justification. Rand is objecting that Aristotle has offered no grounds for exalting those whose example is to serve as the model for virtue.

In response to Rand, it might be replied that Aristotle *does* ask why the *phronimos* acts as he does, answering that he does so because it is fine, since practical wisdom presupposes moral virtue and to act from virtue is in part to act for the sake of the fine (*Nicomachean Ethics* VI.13, 1144a30– 35; III.7, 1115b12, 1116b31; IV.1, 1120a24–25). Further, it might be replied, this is why Aristotle evaluates him so highly. But Rand might respond (and she would not be alone in this worry) that combining these points leads to circularity, or rather makes explicit a circularity that was present all along in Aristotle's view and that was the basis for her charge that he had left certain crucial questions unanswered. If the *phronimos* acts for the sake of the fine, and is to be esteemed on account of this, but is also the standard of what is fine (and thus of what hits the mean and expresses virtue), then we have learned nothing and really do lack a well defined and well-justified ethical standard. Interpretations of Aristotle in this area vary widely and cannot be examined here.[6] But even if Aristotle can be interpreted in a way that avoids the above problem, his ethical theory and his view of practical reasoning have another feature that Rand does not mention but may have worried about and that, in any event, she would be eager to avoid in her own theory of ethics. On Aristotle's view, a rational agent makes eudaimonia or living well his ultimate end and grasps that the fundamental constitutive requirement of living well is "activity of soul in accordance with virtue" (*Nicomachean Ethics* I.7, 1098a7–8) Virtue, in turn, is partly intellectual and partly moral or character-related. The moral virtues are states of character that involve acting with a view to, and for the sake of, what is fine. The concept of the fine is central to Aristotle's account of practical reasoning, for without it the concept of *eudaimonia* would lack rich enough content to yield any specific prescriptions for action; we would be advised to seek to live well without a conception of what living well means.

But the concept of the fine seems to run into the same kind of problems as those which Rand finds in the concept of intrinsic value. Indeed, since recognition of the fine is supposed to be a stopping point in practical deliberation, it seems natural to construe fineness as a kind of intrinsic value (see, for discussion, Korsgaard 1996a, 216–17). What is fine (say, to stand firm in this battle in this way at this time; or to enjoy this form of pleasure at this time to this extent) is so in itself. Further, although the fine is connected with eudaimonia and thus with benefits to the agent who does what is fine, the direction of this connection is the reverse of what Rand thinks it should be. For Rand, properly grounded value claims make the good *of* the agent the standard of what is of value *to* that agent. But for Aristotle, we do not discover what is fine by discovering what we have to do to live well; rather, we discover what we have to do to live well by discovering what is fine, and the fine itself is (he seems to think) intrinsically normative. It is in virtue of doing what is—independently—fine that we also live well. And it is as a result of our being able to flesh out our idea of living well, via a grasp of the fine, that the formally normative notion of "living well" becomes substantively normative, that is, capable of underwriting reasons to do one specific thing rather than another (rather than just whatever it might be that living well involves).

6. See, e.g., McDowell 1980 and McDowell 1995. For a very different account of the same issues, see Charles 1995. Also see the responses to McDowell and Charles by David Wiggins and Stephen Everson, respectively, in Heinaman 1995, 219–31 and 173–99.

Or that at least sometimes appears to be his view. Perhaps there is another way to put the connection between eudaimonia and the fine that makes the fine something other than a kind of intrinsic value. Fineness is a property of intentional human actions; when we ask what is fine, we are asking what is a fine thing for a human being to do. It is plausible to think that, for Aristotle, the answer to this depends on facts about our human nature, since doing what is fine is a form of self-actualization (the criteria for which could hardly be independent of our human nature). Thus, perhaps fine human actions are only fine when they are the actions of human beings; the fine for another species of rational beings might look quite different due to their differences from us. This makes the fineness of fine actions both less intrinsic and more seemingly dependent on a prior conception of human flourishing.

But Aristotle's view is at least ambiguous. Insofar as the fine is supposed to be an independent, intrinsically normative input into a conception of living well, Rand would reject Aristotle's concept of the "fine" as an acceptable basis for ethics or for an account of reasons for action.

Life as an Ultimate Value

Rand needs to explain how reason can give us our ends without relying on (either realist or Kantian) claims of intrinsic value, and how our rational ends can ground reasons for action, including moral reasons. She encapsulates her account as follows: "Life or death is man's only fundamental alternative. To live is his basic act of choice. If he chooses to live, a rational ethics will tell him what principles of action are required to implement his choice. If he chooses not to live, nature will take its course" (*PWNI* 133). Her ethics thus "holds [the requirements of] man's life as the standard of value" and that "[m]an must [i.e., should] choose his actions, values and goals" by this standard "in order to achieve, maintain, fulfill and enjoy that ultimate value, that end in itself, which is his own life" (*VOS* 27). This account thus gives each person a substantively different but formally identical *ultimate value*—his own life. Similarly, it gives each person a substantively different but formally identical ultimate end or goal—to achieve, maintain, fulfill, and enjoy his life.

Rand's formulation of the ultimate end reflects her view of the complexity involved, for human beings as against other species, in valuing our lives. Plants and animals value their lives by acting to maintain them; this is "valuing" in an extended sense of the term, in which one values X insofar as X's attainment or preservation is the goal of one's action. Rand considers this sense of the term applicable to all living things whether or not their goals have the form of conscious (or self-conscious) purposes (see *VOS* 16–17 and for elaboration, see Binswanger 1992). The more complex formulation of the ultimate end for humans suggests that a human being's life is not a given but must be achieved before it can be maintained. Rand's conception of the relation between (human) life and happiness is helpful in explicating this idea: "The maintenance of life and the pursuit of happiness are not two separate issues. . . . Existentially, the activity of pursuing rational goals is the activity of maintaining one's life; psychologically, its result, reward and concomitant is an emotional state of happiness. It is by experiencing happiness that one lives one's life, in any hour, year or the whole of it" (*VOS* 32). What is not given, in the case of humans, are the goals and values, the ongoing pursuit of which figures in this passage as the maintenance of life (and the source of happiness). The sense in which human life is an achievement, according to Rand, is that we must define and choose these goals and values for ourselves. It is these goals and values that constitute one's life or, what comes to the same thing for Rand, that constitute the self.[7] Presumably, this process of choosing values must be somewhat under way before it can become an object of reflection. To self-consciously value life, in that respect which involves achieving it, would then be to take explicit charge of the process— to actively and explicitly deliberate about one's values and goals.

Not only are plants' and animals' lives a given, in the sense that their basic goals and values (in the applicable sense) are biologically fixed

---

7. See *Journals* 78–79 for Rand's view of one's values as constituting one's life and self. I discuss this passage in Wright 2005, 211–13. Allan Gotthelf (2000, 83) has given an excellent explanation of Rand's view that a person's values constitute his life: "The answer [to why this is so] lies in the fact that life is a process of self-sustaining action. The fundamental values that sustain a life will necessarily *constitute* that life." Although Gotthelf offers this with respect to Rand's statement that reason, purpose, and self-esteem are "the means to and the realization of" one's life, he (in my opinion, correctly) does not limit its application to this case. Rand sees all of a person's major values as helping to constitute his life. This is implied in the *Journals* passage cited previously. It is also implicit, for instance, in John Galt's statement in *Atlas Shrugged* that if the national authorities torture Dagny Taggart (the woman he loves) to gain Galt's cooperation, he will kill himself because "there will be no values for me to seek after that, and I do not care to exist without values" (*Atlas* 1091). Though he could exist for a while "in a crippled, disabled . . . condition" (*VOS* 17), Galt's life (as he recognizes) would be over if there were "no values for [him] to seek." Regarding values and the self, see *PWNI*, chapter 5, titled "Selfishness without a Self." In parallel with this chapter title, Rand's novel *We the Living*, which deals, in part, with what happens to a human life when deprived of values, might well have been called "living without a life." Either way, the point is that there is an intolerable and unsustainable incompleteness in a life that lacks values.

rather than chosen, but there is no issue of fulfillment or enjoyment for them to contend with. But these issues loom large for us, and someone who lacked interest in leading a fulfilling and enjoyable life would to that extent be treating his life as unimportant, nonvalued. The *OED* defines to "fulfill" as "[t]o furnish or supply to the full with what is wished for" and "[t]o fill up or make complete,"[8] and Rand includes both of these senses in the aim of fulfilling one's life. The first sense is visible in her claim that the activity of pursuing rational goals—that is, goals one rationally desires—not only maintains one's life but is also the means of achieving happiness, a term that in her usage includes both fulfillment and enjoyment.[9] The second will be visible when we come to a discussion of Rand's analysis of the psychological function of values. On Rand's account, achieving, maintaining, fulfilling, and (thereby) enjoying one's life constitutes one integrated task, in the sense that each of these ends is attained through the same fundamental way of conducting one's life.

With that initial characterization of the ultimate end/value in place, we can turn to the rational grounds for this value as Rand sees them (since the end is specified by reference to the value in the way indicated above, I focus on the ultimate value in what follows). These grounds are to be unearthed by answering a question that Rand considers logically prior to the question of what to value, namely, the question of why one needs values, of what function or purpose they serve in our lives.[10] The basis of this procedure in her thought can be seen in an aspect of her view of the nature of objectivity; she writes, "[o]bjectivity begins with the recognition . . . that there is no room for the arbitrary in any activity of man, least of all in his method of cognition" (*ITOE* 82). By discerning the need for values, she aims to ground value choices that would otherwise be arbitrary. The premise of this approach is that if there is no need for values, we can do without them, and to value one thing over another, or anything at all, will be senseless or irrational. It might be asked whether this reasoning

8. Oxford English Dictionary OED Online, s.v. "Fulfil," http://dictionary.oed.com/entrance.dtl, entries 2 and 3a.

9. Rand characterizes happiness as "that state of consciousness which proceeds from the achievement of one's values" and as "a state of non-contradictory joy—a joy without penalty or guilt, a joy that does not clash with any of your values and does not work for your own destruction, not the joy of escaping from your mind, but of using your mind's fullest power, not the joy of faking reality, but of achieving values that are real, not the joy of a drunkard, but of a producer." See *Atlas* 1014, 1022; cf. *VOS* 31.

10. For her formulation of the issue in terms of the need for values, see *VOS* x, 13–14, and 16; for the same general idea in terms of the function of values, see *VOS* x.

implies that selecting anything (for instance a particular ice cream fla-vor) just because we like it or want it, rather than need it, is arbitrary and senseless. But Rand might reply here that although one probably has no specific need for mint chocolate chip rather than butter pecan, or even any specific need for ice cream, one does (for example) have a need for pleasure, and in innocent and harmless pursuits we achieve pleasure by making choices according to our preferences. In any event, she begins her derivation of a standard of value from the question of why we need values.

Let us begin with a fairly abstract, structural consideration of this procedure. If one needs values just in order to φ, then the requirements of φ-ing will (Rand argues) be the proper standard of value and φ itself will be the proper ultimate value. It will be "proper," however, in the sense of being that which one has to gain by pursuing values. Suppose there is some outcome, ψ, in relation to which valuing makes no difference (e.g., a certain star's burning out over a certain period of time). Then, Rand would argue, it would be senseless and unjustified to try to select values by reference to this outcome, since the requirements for its coming to pass would imply nothing about valuing and, by hypothesis, could be satis-fied even if we had no values. By contrast, if one needs values (precisely) in order to φ, it would make sense to select values according to φ, since that is just what one stands to gain (or not) depending on the values one selected and the actions one took in the service of those values.[11] Accord-ing to Rand, that gives φ a rational claim to be the standard of value. But, crucially, in her view it does not yet give φ any rational claim on one's actions. To put this differently, Rand argues that although one's needing values (precisely) in order to φ makes φ normative for valuing, it does not make φ intrinsically normative.

In explicating Rand's view so far, I have focused on the arbitrariness she sees in an attempt to select values apart from the question of why they are needed. But in addition to this epistemic claim, she also makes a psychological claim: the issue of selecting values could not even arise for us—we couldn't grasp it as an issue—if we had nothing at stake in it.

11. I'm assuming that if one needs values to φ, then one needs certain values and not just any values to do so, and thus that φ would supply a standard of correctness for one's value selections. If what φ-ing required were simply any values, whatever they were, then it would still provide a minimal sort of standard by which having values would be justified if one had the end of φ-ing. But it would not provide the sort of standard that Rand is seeking, one that discriminates among different candidate values. The argument Rand makes can only succeed if we need values for an end that requires some values and not others, which, as we will see, is the position that she defends.

To illustrate this, Rand proposes a thought experiment involving a robot that "cannot be affected by anything" nor "changed in any respect" and so "cannot be damaged, injured or destroyed." She comments: "Such an entity would not be able to have any values; it would have nothing to gain or to lose; it could not regard anything as *for* or *against* it, as serving or threatening its welfare, as fulfilling or frustrating its interests. It could have no interests and no goals" (*VOS* 16). The point here is not just that this entity would not be able to decide what to value, but that the concept of a value would be one that it could not even form, not even in an implicit, inchoate way. It would have no sense of things as better or worse than one another, nor any incentive to target its actions on some objects rather than others.

By contrast, we can have values because we *can* be affected by things, changed, damaged, injured, or destroyed. Rand expresses this point by saying that we, unlike the robot, face alternatives that make it both possible and necessary for us to form and pursue values. Facing an alternative, in the relevant sense, involves more than being faced by what we might call "external alternatives," such as sun or rain, world peace or global conflict. The robot, as Rand describes it, has no basis for taking interest in the outcomes of alternatives like these because of the invariability of its own internal condition. What is needed for facing an alternative in the sense relevant to having values is the presence of some internal alternative, that is, something at stake in one's own internal condition that can give one a stake in how things stand externally. Further, there needs to be a connection between one's internal condition and one's action; it needs to be the case that the outcome of the internal alternatives confronting one depends on how one acts. Both of these conditions are fulfilled in our own case: our own internal condition is variable and depends on our action. Because we face action-sensitive, internal alternatives, we also face external alternatives in a stronger sense than the robot: we face external alternatives that can make a difference to us—that can bear on our internal condition and thus also provide grounds for the formation of values.

In these respects, we face a common predicament with all living organisms: every organism must act in order to maintain itself; it faces alternatives with respect to its own well-being that generate the occasion and need for goal-directed action. Goal-directness in nonconscious organisms like plants is, of course, not purposeful. Plant teleology (e.g., a plant's growing roots in order to draw nutrients from the soil, or turning its leaves toward the sun in order to catch sunlight) is not plant intentionality. But in a broad sense the things that a plant's teleological action targets (e.g., sunlight, nutrients) are values that it acts for and are of value to it in relation to the ends for which it needs those things (and to which they are indeed conducive). They are values in the sense that they are objects of a living organism's goal-directed action; the same is true of the things targeted by the teleological action of animals. Rand's most general definition of a "value," "that which one acts to gain and/or keep" (VOS 16), is deliberately broad enough to encompass these cases.

According to Rand, the fact that we face internal, action-sensitive alternatives is what makes it both possible and necessary for us to form values. The necessity here is conditional: we must do so if we are to affect the outcome of the internal alternatives we face. But for Rand, the process of value formation has more structure than this initial formulation might imply. She holds that every living organism confronts one basic alternative that underlies all the other alternatives that it faces, specifically, that of the existence or non-existence of the organism's own life:

> There is one fundamental alternative in the universe: existence or nonexistence—and it pertains to a single class of entities: to living organisms. The existence of inanimate matter is unconditional, the existence of life is not: it depends on a specific course of action. Matter is indestructible, it changes its forms, but it cannot cease to exist. It is only a living organism that faces a constant alternative: the issue of life or death. Life is a process of self-sustaining and self-generated action. If an organism fails in that action, it dies; its chemical elements remain, but its life goes out of existence. (VOS 16 [quoted from Atlas 1012–13])

The preservation of the organism itself is, of course, the same thing as the preservation of its life; once the organism's life is gone, the organism itself is gone (qua living organism—qua what it is—though "its chemical elements remain"). Rand's view is that all the values that an organism needs are needed for the sake of maintaining its life or, what comes to the same thing, for the sake of itself—its own self-preservation. The organism's self or life thus functions as its ultimate value in relation to which other values come into view as values. And these other values come into view only as values for the organism that needs them. Thus, "[t]he concept of value is not a primary; it presupposes an answer to the question: of value to *whom* and for *what*?" (VOS 16). The kind of value ascription that it will be possible (justifiably) to make will have the form: V is of value to O for the sake (ultimately) of O's life. There will (in principle) be an intelligible, objective basis for statements of this form in the nature and needs of the different species of living things.[12]

We might wonder whether this general model of goal-directed action as geared toward the maintenance of an organism's life, whatever merit it may have in regard to nonhumans, is applicable without modification to human beings. Even in the case of nonhumans, it has been a matter of debate whether goal-directed action in living things is exclusively directed at the individual acting organism's own survival. The issue turns in part on whether an organism that is biologically programmed to take certain risks or bear certain costs for the benefit of other members of the same population gains a net survival advantage from the similar programming of (some of) those other members.[13]

But there is a different issue to consider in the case of human beings. Members of nonhuman species need values but not moral values, whereas Rand holds that the requirements of man's life are the correct standard not just for selecting generic human values but for defining a moral code. And so we should consider some of what she says about the relation between life and morality.

Life and Morality

An argument that morality is needed in order to live may seem like a nonstarter. But Rand's description of "the activity of pursuing rational goals" as "the activity of maintaining one's life" and her denial that maintaining one's life and pursuing happiness are "separate issues" should alert us that there is more to the argument than might be expected. She argues, "[t]o hold one's own life as one's highest value, and one's own happiness as one's highest purpose are two aspects of the same achievement" (*VOS* 32). That an ethics of virtue could be in the offing here now looks less surprising.[14] Grounding virtues in the requirements of happiness or flourishing,

12. Applying this perspective to the case of human values, Rand writes: "Values cannot exist (cannot be valued) outside the full context of a man's life, needs, goals, and *knowledge*" (*CUI* 16). Thus, values are brought into existence as values by an act of valuing, and an act of valuing is an intellectual act that (when properly performed) draws on a wide context of the valuer's knowledge, including (but not limited to) knowledge about his life, needs, and goals.

13. For an affirmative argument on this question, in the spirit of Rand's philosophy, see Binswanger 1990.

14. Unlike some virtue theorists, Rand does not put emphasis on the distinction between "morality" and "ethics." She uses the terms as synonyms (see *VOS* 13), and although she frames her central moral norms as virtues, she is equally at home with the language of

however, has proven a daunting task in other theories, and Rand takes it on in an especially challenging form, since she wants to argue not only that we cannot flourish or be happy without morality but that, in the long term, we cannot even survive.

Perhaps Rand's most perspicuous explanation of why man needs morality comes in the following passage:

> Just as man's physical survival depends on his own effort, so does his psychological survival. Man faces two corollary, interdependent fields of action in which a constant exercise of choice and a constant creative process are demanded of him: the world around him and his own soul. . . . Just as he has to produce the material values he needs to sustain his life, so he has to acquire the values of character that enable him to sustain it and that make his life worth living. He is born without the knowledge of either. He has to discover both—and translate them into reality—and survive by shaping the world and himself in the image of his values. (*RM* 163)

Values of character, which I take to be moral values,[15] are at the center of this passage. We need them, the passage tells us, both to enable us to sustain our lives and to make life worth living for us. Survival, then, turns out to be a process of acting under the guidance of our moral (and other) values, to shape the world and to shape our individual moral character (see also *Atlas* 1020–21). The passage speaks of two kinds of survival: physical and psychological. Physical survival clearly depends on material values as well as on one's moral values in that these, Rand says, enable one to create the material values one needs.[16] Psychological survival depends

---

morality, narrowly conceived as involving obligations, laws, and rights. (See, e.g., *VOS* chap. 12, esp. 108–9, and *PWNI*, chap. 10, esp. 128–29, 133, and 136.) She does not, of course, accept the prevailing conception of morality as an essentially impartial mode of practical evaluation that gives no special weight to the moral agent's own interests. Although in the text I loosely refer to her normative theory as an "ethics of virtue," the blending of ethical and narrowly moral concepts in her theory sets it apart from at least many theories in virtue ethics and is one reason against placing her theory in this category.

15. See *VOS* 29, where the treatment of values of character as moral values (and virtues) is explicit.

16. In a division of labor society, then, one would also depend (according to Rand's account) on the moral character of those with whom one trades, which illustrates one sense in which Rand holds that one has an interest in the good moral character of others. But she would argue that one depends fundamentally on one's own character, since that will ultimately determine what one will have to offer others in trade. See, for related discussion, *VOS*, chap. 4.

directly on one's own moral character.[17] Rand, I believe, would also say that each of these aspects of our survival depends on other values, such as philosophy (philosophical knowledge), science, art (see *RM* 162–63), and many others, and that there are various cross-dependencies. (For example, in one place she depicts psychological survival as depending on certain material values; see her charming example of the stenographer who buys lipstick, *CUI* 17.) But for present purposes the foregoing suffices to indicate in broad terms the sense in which Rand claims that we need moral values in order to survive.

Although it may be clear in a general way how developing values of character could help make one's life worth living, by giving one a sense of pride, Rand's use of the term "psychological survival" is less transparent. The term is unusual, and it reflects one of the most important and distinctive aspects of her thought, her view of the role of human consciousness in survival. Psychological survival refers to one's survival as a valuer, as someone who has something to live for. Rand insists that human consciousness, as a biological capacity, cannot function if its needs are not fulfilled: "Man's consciousness is his least known and most abused vital organ. Most people believe that consciousness as such is some sort of indeterminate faculty which has no *nature,* no specific identity, and, therefore, no requirements, no needs, no rules for being properly or improperly used. The simplest example of this belief is people's willingness to lie or cheat, to fake reality on the premise that 'I'm the only one who'll know' or 'It's only in my mind'—without any concern for what this does to one's mind, what complex, untraceable, disastrous impairments it produces, what crippling damage may result" (*VOR* 101).

Moreover, the central needs of human consciousness include values, which "are the motivating power of man's actions and a *necessity* of his survival, psychologically as well as physically." The absence of values puts psychological survival in danger: "A chronic lack of pleasure, of any enjoyable, rewarding or stimulating experiences, produces a slow, gradual, day-by-day erosion of man's emotional vitality, which he may ignore or repress, but which is recorded by the relentless computer of his subconscious mechanism that registers an ebbing flow, then a trickle, then a few last drops of fuel—until the day when his inner motor stops and he won-

---

17. Whether or not she thinks it depends on other people's moral character, and if so to what extent, is an interesting question. This seems to have been the intended concern of a planned fifth novel, *To Lorne Dieterling,* which Rand never completed. See *Journals* 706–15.

ders desperately why he has no desire to go on, unable to find any definable cause of his hopeless, chronic sense of exhaustion" (*VOR* 104).

Value-deprivation can have external sources, in Rand's view, such as a bleak, nihilistic cultural environment. But it can also have inner causes, in the pursuit of irrational substitutes for genuinely "enjoyable, rewarding or stimulating experiences," substitutes that would not actually satisfy our need for such experiences. It is possible to discover that something one had regarded as a value leaves one empty, conflicted, or anxiety-ridden; that one's standards of value were distorting and the projected rewards were illusory. This is the situation of Rand's character Peter Keating in *The Fountainhead*, who seeks approval and prestige above all else in life, but slowly loses the will to go on (see *Fountainhead* pt. IV, chaps. 7–10 and chap. 14).

Rand's normative ethics is centered on the three "cardinal [moral] values" of reason, purpose, and self-esteem, which "are the means to and the realization of one's ultimate value, one's own life" (*VOS* 27). Corresponding to these are (respectively) the virtues of rationality, productiveness, and pride (*VOS* 27). To value reason is to use it and thus to demonstrate rationality in thought and action. To value purpose is to live a purposeful life, which, Rand argues, requires a commitment to productive work as one's central life concern. To value self-esteem—the conviction that one is able to live and worthy of living—requires becoming able and worthy, which, Rand argues, requires a commitment to leading a moral life (a commitment she equates with pride, understood as a virtue rather than as a vice). Rand presents four other virtues as aspects of rationality: honesty, independence, integrity, and justice. Here I focus only on the three cardinal virtues, in order to illuminate the basic way in which she sees the requirements of survival as grounding a code of morality.

Let us begin from Rand's view of the relationship of moral virtue to physical survival. "Everything man needs," Rand writes, "has to be discovered by his own mind and produced by his own effort." A human being:

> cannot provide for his simplest physical needs without a process of thought. He needs a process of thought to discover how to plant and grow his food or how to make weapons for hunting. His percepts might lead him to a cave, if one is available—but to build the simplest shelter, he needs a process of thought. No percepts and no "instincts" will tell him how to light a fire, how to weave cloth, how to forge tools, how to make a wheel, how to make an airplane, how to perform an appendectomy, how

to produce an electric light bulb or an electronic tube or a cyclotron or a box of matches. Yet his life depends on such knowledge—and only a volitional act of his consciousness, a process of thought, can provide it. (*VOS* 25)

As a consequence, thinking and productive work are "the two essentials" (*VOS* 25) of our long-term physical survival. Free riders, those who merely imitate or expropriate the independent thought and work of others, put their long-term survival at risk: the imitator may select the wrong models; the exploiter, in the long run, hampers and destroys those on whose support he depends. In Rand's view, however, free riding also carries a near-term (and lasting) psychological penalty. Free riding is a low-effort substitute for developing one's own intellectual resources—one's own ability to think and to create the sorts of values that our lives require, whether material values like food and shelter, spiritual values like art, intellectual values such as new scientific discoveries or job efficiencies, or others. These sorts of values enable one to be self-supporting, either directly or through trade with other productive individuals. But, Rand writes, "[t]he choice to think or not is volitional. If an individual's choice is predominantly negative, the result is his self-arrested mental development, a self-made cognitive malnutrition, a stagnant, eroded, impoverished, anxiety-ridden inner life" (*VOS* 102). The free rider cannot avoid psychological suffering, a sense of helplessness, and a sense that life offers him or her nothing worth living for, according to Rand. By contrast, she maintains, the thinker and producer develops a sense of competence and mastery in the areas in which he exerts his efforts and develops specific personal values, centering on a career, that require a long-term focus and give meaning to life as a whole. Further, Rand holds, because these attainments flow from a person's own choices, he develops a sense of self-esteem; by contrast, the free rider's dependence on others deprives that person of self-esteem.

The need for self-esteem, on Rand's view, is an aspect of the need to experience one's life as worth living. This need can be seen as having two aspects: the need to experience life as having something to offer one, and the need to experience oneself as a worthy beneficiary of what life has to offer. If Rand is right, then what life preeminently has to offer us are the psychological rewards of thinking and productive work (the rewards of human relationships are crucially important, in her view, but depend on one's having some purpose in life that is independent of those relationships; see, e.g., *Fountainhead* 386–88). But for those rewards to be accessible to us, we must fit ourselves to receive them by actually taking the initiative to develop our minds, to find work that absorbs us, to acquire the skills needed for it, and to pursue a career. Since our experiencing life as having something to offer depends on our own initiative, it is attributable to our own choices and therefore provides grounds for a sense of self-worth. The lack of self-esteem, in Rand's view, is a psychological impediment to action: "Every act of man's life has to be willed; the mere act of obtaining or eating his food implies that the person he preserves is worthy of being preserved; every pleasure he seeks to enjoy implies that the person who seeks it is worthy of finding enjoyment" (*Atlas* 1057).

Self-contempt, therefore, undermines us psychologically: a view of oneself as unworthy renders the pursuit of values pointless, even unjustifiable. But, Rand argues, "to lose your ambition for values is to lose your ambition to live" (*Atlas* 1020). If self-esteem is a necessary condition of the preservation of this ambition, then it is a necessary condition of being able to live. And this is just how Rand views it: "By a feeling he has not learned to identify, but has derived from his first awareness of existence, from his discovery that he has to make choices, man knows that his desperate need of self-esteem is a matter of life or death. As a being of volitional consciousness, he knows that he must know his own value in order to maintain his own life. He knows that he has to be *right*; to be wrong in action means danger to his life; to be wrong in person, to be *evil*, means to be unfit for existence" (*Atlas* 1056–57).

In view of her conception of the role of thinking and productive work in our physical and psychological self-sustenance, Rand identifies rationality and productiveness as cardinal moral virtues. "Rationality," as she characterizes it, involves a commitment to the development of one's mind, to the full and consistent use of reason in forming one's convictions and guiding one's action, and thus to not acting merely on the prompting of unanalyzed emotions. "Productiveness" involves both the commitment to seeking work through which to sustain oneself psychologically and physically—thus the effort to develop one's interests and abilities—and the commitment to treating one's work as a career and doing it as intelligently and creatively as one can. In view of our need for self-esteem, Rand identifies pride as the third cardinal moral virtue. We maintain our self-esteem, according to Rand, by becoming and remaining psychologically and existentially "fit for existence"—fit to engage in and draw fulfillment from the rational and productive activities that also serve to provide for our material needs. On Rand's account, attaining this condition requires the moral virtues of rationality and productiveness. She therefore concludes that self-esteem derives from the maintenance of an overriding commitment to morality: "[T]he first precondition of self-esteem is that radiant selfishness of soul which desires the best in all things, in values of matter and spirit, a soul that seeks above all else to achieve its own moral perfection" (*Atlas* 1021). It is this condition of soul that constitutes pride, and Rand therefore maintains that this virtue, like rationality and productiveness, is one that we need in order to live.

This foregoing sketch of Rand's ethical theory was aimed at clarifying the sense in which, for Rand, life is the goal of morality. There is, of course, much more to be said on each of the topics I have touched on. But I now want to return to the former discussion of her derivation of a standard of value and raise two further issues. One involves a closer consideration of the step in Rand's argument from the identification of a basic alternative to the justification of an ultimate value. The other arises from Rand's view that valuing one's life is a choice and concerns the implication of this view for her account of moral obligation.

Justifying an Ultimate Value

Rand's argument for an ultimate value moves from the premise that we face the basic alternative of existence or non-existence to the conclusion that a person's ultimate value should be his own life. By definition, an alternative presents one with two or more possible pathways, but the mere existence of multiple pathways does not usually settle the question of which one of them an agent ought to take; on the contrary, it usually raises this question, since the question could not arise if there were only one way to go. Yet Rand seems to treat the fundamentality of her basic alternative not as raising a question about what to seek but as settling this question. The fundamentality of the basic alternative is supposed to show that one's own life is the proper ultimate value by which to evaluate other prospective values and courses of action. In other cases where we are presented with alternatives, a further step is required: we must find a criterion for selecting among our alternatives. But in this case, it seems, we are to proceed straight from the identification of the basic alternative to a decision in favor of one side of this alternative.

The need for a special procedure in regard to the basic alternative is clear. On Rand's view, the decision between other alternatives is to be made by seeing what further value is at stake. For instance, if her arguments about the need for productiveness are correct, then one should resolve the alternative of being productive or unproductive by reference to the way in which productiveness serves one's life (one's deliberation on this being mediated by general knowledge of the way in which productiveness serves the life of any human being as such, plus the fact that one is oneself a human being). But if we are presented with a basic alternative (in Rand's sense), then no further value can be at stake for us depending on how we resolve the basic alternative, for then the alternative would not after all be basic. A basic alternative, for Rand, is precisely one whose resolution has no further impact on the agent confronting it other than the impact of its being resolved one way or the other; thus Rand's view is that what an organism has at stake in the continuation or discontinuation of its life is simply the continuation or discontinuation of its life. That, of course, includes the continuation or discontinuation of all the actions and processes that make up the organism's life. But there is nothing else, in Rand's view—nothing over and above everything that comprises the organism's life—that the organism has at stake depending on whether or not its life continues.

Moving from a basic alternative to an ultimate value thus requires a special procedure. The only procedure that will not defeat Rand's purposes is the truncated one she follows (it should be clear by now that calling in an intrinsic value, for instance, would be completely self-defeating for Rand). Rand's inference from her basic alternative to one's life as one's ultimate value depends on a distinctive feature of the basic alternative, in contrast with other alternatives. Like any alternative, this one presents us with a slate (in this case, a pair) of possible outcomes. In the basic alternative, however, only one of the outcomes corresponds to a value, that is, to something that is a candidate for being valued. The candidate value is one's life. On one side of the alternative, this value is sustained; on the other side, it isn't. But there is no second value offered on this latter side of the alternative, only the absence both of value and valuer. There's nothing one passes up in valuing one's life and thus no choice among possible values to be made. There is, in Rand's view, a choice involved in valuing one's life; this isn't automatic, at least not once a person reaches the stage of being able to make self-conscious value choices. But the identification of the basic alternative enables us in Rand's view to make a judgment straight away as to the ultimate value one should hold if one values anything at all.

There is, I think, one last point to note. It is important to Rand's argument that she show that life or death is a genuinely fundamental alternative, and that involves showing that one's life can serve as its own end. If we could not make sense of the idea of valuing life for its own sake, then the issue of whether life or death was our basic alternative would have to be reopened. Rand is clearly aware of this point, writing that "[m]etaphysically life is the only phenomenon that is an end in itself: a value gained and kept by a constant process of action"(*VOS* 18). Because she sees life as requiring a constant process of action, including the action needed for psychological survival, she views the maintenance of life as an all-embracing task; there is no setting it aside and no getting outside of it or beyond it. The point of this characterization of life as requiring constant action seems to be precisely to emphasize the way in which living serves the end of living further and thus is its own end. This would not be plausible, however, if Rand had understood maintaining one's life exclusively in terms of physical survival. Indeed, Rand's concept of value deprivation serves to highlight that physical survival alone cannot be one's ultimate end.

Choice, Morality, and Reasons for Action

Although ethics, for Rand, is egoistic—the moral virtues are delineated by reference to the requirements of the virtuous agent's own life[18]—Rand is not a psychological egoist. She does not hold that we are psychologically programmed to value our lives or strive to further them, and a person who values his life to some extent may not value his life as an end or as an ultimate end. Nor, as we have seen, does Rand defend a categorical requirement either of rationality or morality to value our lives (at all or as an ultimate end). On her view, valuing one's life (and holding it as an ultimate value) is a choice, and all reasons for action, including moral reasons, arise in relation to the choice to value one's life (the choice to live) (*PWNI* 133). Since a certain moral code (she argues) is needed in order to live, the choice to live gives rise to certain moral obligations, and these

---

18. It should be noted that Rand does not hold the standard form of "ethical egoism," on which the maximal furtherance of the agent's self-interest is taken as the *criterion* of moral rightness. Rand would have the same objection to this view as she has to its hedonistic analogue, the view that takes happiness as a moral criterion. Her objection to the latter is that morality is needed to define the requirements of happiness, that is, to define a rational code of values whose implementation can enable a person to achieve happiness (see *VOS* 32–33). Similarly, she argues that morality is needed to "define and determine [man's] actual self-interest" (*VOS* x, see also xi).

obligations are reason-giving. Further, on Rand's view of the fundamental role of morality in enabling the creation and preservation of the broad range of other values one's life depends on, moral reasons define the space of possibilities within which further rational deliberation about action can occur and in which other kinds of practical reasons can emerge. But the choice to live itself is not subject to moral deliberation; it precedes and sets the context for moral deliberation (see *Atlas* 1018).

The exact nature of the link between reasons/obligations and the choice to live bears further examination. This is a large topic and I will only scratch the surface of it here. Because of the way in which Rand links reasons for action with the choice to live, her view seems to imply that someone who does not value his life lacks any reason to be moral. One might then wonder whether such a person is thereby released from all moral obligations, a conclusion that is hard to accept.[19] Further, Rand seems to judge people negatively for not valuing their lives or not valuing them highly enough. Someone who was highly self-sacrificing would presumably fall into this category. But in Rand's view, self-sacrifice is immoral, rather than premoral or in some other way outside the scope of moral deliberation (see *VOS*, chap. 3, esp. 52). There are individuals, such as suicide terrorists, who could only be described as patently life-hating, obsessed with destroying themselves and innocent others. It would be hard to view them as choosing to live, and yet it seems equally as unacceptable to hold that they have no moral obligations, as if their nihilism were a moral dispensation. Moreover, their failure to value life seems to be the root of what is morally wrong with them.

Now there is at least one clear sense in which the individuals in these examples, and their actions, do come within the scope of morality on Rand's view. Moral obligations, she holds, are to be delineated according to the abstract standard of "man's life"—the requirements of maintaining, fulfilling, and enjoying one's life that can be derived from the nature of human life as such. If her arguments about the foundations of morality are correct, then there is exactly one set of moral standards that can be justified as rational and correct. Rand's standards include, for example, respecting innocent life and not being self-sacrificing, therefore, the actions of suicide terrorists and self-sacrificing people conflict with the only

19. Allan Gotthelf considers this issue in his 1990 Ayn Rand Society presentation on "The Choice to Value" (which also appears in the present volume). One can see him struggling to avoid this conclusion in a part of the paper with which, he reports, he no longer agrees.

justifiable morality and thus can properly be evaluated as morally wrong. Further, these agents themselves and their motives will in principle be morally evaluable (e.g., as vicious, evil, immoral, etc.—I leave aside what precise form these evaluations would take and what criteria would warrant them).

This sounds like a form of moral externalism, on which morality may not give all agents reasons for action, although moral descriptions of agents and their actions are applicable across the board in the minimal sense that their criteria of application are independent of an agent's reasons.[20] In the above examples, the actions taken would be correctly describable, from the standpoint of Rand's moral theory, as "morally wrong." But could the agents be said to have any moral obligations? They might be said to have moral obligations, obligations under the system of morality that the theory presents as correct (and that is correct, if the theory is true). But that seems analogous to saying that a person has an obligation to pay us some money under a contract he didn't sign. Although this might be true, the person would not on that account actually owe us anything. Rand traces oughts to the choice to live, and that seems to suggest that those who do not make this choice do not have obligations. Here it is worth noting that on her account, it is not the case that such individuals can have other reasons that supplant or override moral reasons. To the extent that they lack moral reasons, they lack any reasons to act one way as opposed to another; they lack what in Rand's view is the condition of reason-guided action, a commitment to the value of their own lives.

It might be supposed that merely taking action amounts to choosing to live, and thus that anyone who acts at all has moral reasons. But that clearly isn't Rand's view, as, for example, the character of James Taggart in *Atlas Shrugged* illustrates (*Atlas* 1144–45). Taggart has a hatred of existence and would rather destroy himself than see others succeed. For Rand, he represents one possible kind of case of someone's not choosing to live, although presumably not a typical case. I will not pursue here the question of how widespread she considers the failure to choose to live, or in what other forms that failure could manifest itself. Certainly Rand is no existentialist; she does not hold that it is psychologically possible for the average person (or any reasonably mentally healthy person) at any moment to leap to death from the roof of a building or shoot a gun

20. For a clear recent account of the contrasts among this and other forms of externalism and internalism in ethics, see Tresan 2009.

pointed at his own temple. There do seem to be cases quite different from the Taggart case in which a person confronts an overtly existential decision, one that involves, on its face, a choice about whether or not to value one's life (for example, if someone has reached a stage of drug addiction at which further drug use will kill him, as in the film *Half Nelson*). But I leave aside for now the issue of what, in principle, the choice to live (or its absence) involves.

Returning to the issues of moral obligation, the case of Taggart is instructive in another way. Rand's attitude toward him is not neutral, as it might be if she considered the choice to live to be non-evaluable and those who do not make this choice to be free of moral obligations. She calls the choice to live a basic choice. A neutral attitude may seem warranted (given that characterization) if we think of a basic choice as one for which there are no deliberative grounds. But that inference is hasty. For there might be other grounds that are not brought to bear through deliberation. Rand rejects the attribution of intrinsic value to life, and thus would reject an account of the choice to live as proceeding from the deliberative recognition of such value. But she also holds that it is possible to directly experience one's life as a value. For instance, in the sequel to a passage examined earlier, she writes, "when one experiences the kind of pure happiness that is an end in itself—the kind that makes one think: '*This* is worth living for'—what one is greeting and affirming in emotional terms is the metaphysical fact that *life* is an end in itself" (*VOS* 32). Similarly, the experience of certain forms of art provides "the life-giving fact of experiencing a moment of metaphysical joy—a moment of love for existence" (*RM* 163). Expressing a view he drew from Rand, Nathaniel Branden broadens the point: "Through the state of enjoyment, man experiences the value of life, the sense that life is worth living, worth struggling to maintain. . . . Thus, in letting man experience, in his own person, the sense that *life* is a value and that *he* is a value, pleasure serves as the emotional fuel of man's existence" (*VOS* 71).

That some people who are very badly off can still manage, at times, to feel joy and to experience life as a value, and to struggle against obstacles, I think shows that these sorts of experiences need not wait on great good luck. This makes it hard to take a neutral view of the sorts of people we were contemplating above, people who at a fundamental level do not value their lives, and it may explain why Rand is not neutral toward Taggart. If it is not particularly hard to experience one's life as a value, then there are easily accessible nondeliberative grounds for making the choice to value one's life.[21] The choice goes beyond the experience; it is a response to the experience that involves forming certain kinds of intentions, which set an agenda for moral reflection and action in support of one's life. The existence of nondeliberative grounds for the choice also supplies justification for a negative verdict on those who (again, in some fundamental way, rather than due to evil circumstances) do not value their lives. From Rand's perspective, they are rightly seen as abominable.[22] Given the connection she draws between morality and life, would she also regard them as subject to moral judgment, by extension? It seems to me that she cannot say there is anything such people have a moral reason, or any kind of reason, to do, if she is to retain the connection between reasons/obligations and the choice to live. But I do not think it follows that she is restricted to making external judgments only. There may be nothing that someone who does not value his life has a moral reason to do. Nevertheless, such a person can be morally evil not only in an externalist sense that the description correctly applies to him or her, but in the sense that the description corresponds to a real defect or corruption in that person traceable to a groundless rejection of life. From this perspective, the lack of moral reasons would figure as an additional deficiency instead of as an exculpation.

Other Interpretations of Rand on Obligation and Choice

The interpretation given in the preceding section differs from two other interpretations discussed in the literature on Rand. The first is what Douglas Rasmussen has called the "voluntarist" interpretation (see 2002, 81–83, also 72–73; and see 2006, 310–12 and 324–25, where he refers to a similar view as "the official doctrine"). This interpretation holds that the choice to live is absolutely fundamental, in the sense that: (a) there are no normative grounds for making it or not making it; (b) it is not subject to any form of evaluation (as rational, moral, etc.); (c) the agent making (or not making) this choice is not subject to any form of evaluation qua making (or not making) it. Rasmussen criticizes this interpretation; more specifically, he rejects the claim that Rand unambiguously holds the vol-

21. By "nondeliberative grounds" for this choice, I mean a cognitive input that occasions the choice, and to which the choice is an intelligible and rational response, but which does not have propositional content.

22. The account sketched in this paragraph clearly requires elaboration and defense, both as a view and as interpretation of Rand. I have offered what I take to be some initial textual basis for attributing it to Rand, although given space constraints I cannot defend the interpretation fully here.

untarist view (though he thinks she sometimes suggests it), and he rejects the claim that it is a plausible view in its own right. His own view—which he also sees some reason for ascribing to Rand—is that, for any agent, his own life is something that is "choiceworthy, something that [he] ought to choose" (2002, 82). On this view, an agent's own life and the necessary means of sustaining the agent's life have self-standing "directive power" (82) for that agent's actions, regardless of the agent's choices (see also 2006, 315).

Though he attempts to distinguish his view from the kind of "intrinsicism" that Rand would clearly have rejected, it is difficult to see what the distinction is. On Rasmussen's view, one's life has directive power because it is one's ultimate *good*. Certainly, on Rasmussen's view, this good is agent-relative in the sense that it is one's own life rather than, say, life as such, that constitutes an agent's good. But according to Rasmussen, this good is still prescribed for one as one's telos, independently of one's choices, by virtue of one's nature as a living being (2006, 314, 315). It is therefore difficult to support the ascription of this kind of position to Rand, given her clear statement that prescriptions for action arise in relation to the choice to live. Although Rasmussen believes that the rejection of his position leads to voluntarism, I have tried to sketch a coherent third alternative that Rand's texts would seem to support.

The way that Rasmussen (2002) interprets Rand depends heavily on a certain way of reading her statement that "Metaphysically, *life* is the only phenomenon that is an end in itself" and the argument leading up to that statement in "The Objectivist Ethics" (see *VOS* 16–18). Rasmussen takes Rand to be treating life as a natural (ultimate) end, an end that human nature marks out as one to be pursued for its own sake and as the ultimate goal of all of one's action. We can see that life has this status, he argues, by analyzing the relationship between choice and value. Choice does not create value; rather choice exists for the sake of value and ultimately for the sake of the value of life. That is, when we ask what the function of choice is for volitional beings such as ourselves, we find that its function is to promote life (and, more immediately, the values whose realization life depends on) (see 2002, 74–76).

But there are at least two problems with this way of reading Rand. First, it misconstrues her point about life's being metaphysically an end. Her full statement is as follows: "Metaphysically, *life* is the only phenomenon that is an end in itself: a value gained and kept by a constant process of action" (*VOS* 18). The point here is that since life must be continuously gained and kept, the realization of this value does not lead to any further values to which it is a means. To say this is not to hold that one ought to live, but rather to hold that only one's life can serve as the ultimate goal of all one's other values, which is not the same thing. Second, although Rand does refer to the "function of values" in the introduction to *The Virtue of Selfishness* (*VOS* x)—and although we might also see her as ascribing a certain function to choice—Rasmussen does not analyze the way in which Rand uses the term "function," a term that is liable to a number of different construals. In practice during the course of the argument of "The Objectivist Ethics," Rand takes the function of a thing (for example, values) to be that for which it is needed. In *Introduction to Objectivist Epistemology* she says (less satisfactorily in my view) that the function of a thing is "what the thing can do or what you can do with it" (*ITOE* 210). On neither usage does it follow straight away, from X's having function F, that one is obligated to use X for F or that one is obligated to seek F.

It should be noted that the interpretation of Rand that I defend above does not attribute to her the implausible view that the function of human choice depends on human choice, a view that Rasmussen associates with what he calls the "orthodox" interpretation (see 2006, 313). Similarly, my interpretation does not ascribe to Rand the view that the standards by which we should evaluate values and choices are chosen by us. They must of course be identified by us, but according to Rand it is facts about reality and human nature that make it the case that certain standards are the correct ones.

Rasmussen (2002) also argues as follows: If life has no choice-independent "directive power" for one's actions, then why should one choose the means to life? More broadly, why should one choose the means to any of one's ends if none of those ends has directive power independent of one's choices? If we answer that life acquires directive power when we choose it, there are two problems. How does our choosing it give it directive power? And what does our choice amount to if we are not choosing life in virtue of its directive power? Our choice, then, seems like no choice at all but merely a happening that comes out of nowhere (see 2002, 82–83).

As mentioned above, Rasmussen attempts to solve these problems by arguing that life is "choiceworthy, something that we ought to choose" (2002, 82). The slide from the first description to the second is interesting, since there seems to be a gap between them: many things could be considered choiceworthy that are in no way obligatory (e.g., a certain vacation destination). And, in a rather different sense than Rasmussen intends, we might even describe Rand as holding that it is possible to experience one's life as "choiceworthy" and thereby to have a reason for choosing to live. But, importantly, when one finds life to be something choiceworthy, it is from the perspective of one who is already actively involved in it, and in part it is that active involvement that makes it choiceworthy. One comes to find life choiceworthy as a result of having sought out and achieved values within it. It is thus choiceworthy—to use that terminology—qua already chosen. Similarly, one chooses to live while already engaged in that process. In each case, one is ratifying—and making conscious, consistent, and comprehensive—one's commitment to a value or an activity that one has already to some extent embraced in a less reflective way. This seems like quite a different thing from grasping that it is one's telos to live and then doing so on that account. In any event, on the view I have sketched, one's less reflectively attained narrower values—the disparate kinds of values a person normally develops in the course of growing up—enable one to experience one's life as being a value. At a later stage of moral reflection (assuming one reaches it), one is in a position to make a choice to strive fully and consistently to maintain and fulfill one's life as an ultimate end. And one's reasons for doing so would at this point be threefold: the value one attaches to one's own life; the understanding (if Rand's account of the foundations of value is correct) that it is only this value that makes one's other values possible and necessary; the understanding (if Rand's moral psychology is correct) that one must choose to hold one's life as an ultimate value if one is to consistently maintain and fulfill it—that, for a human being, living is not an automatic process.

For Rand, then, in sum, life is normative for valuing but not intrinsically normative, and her defense of life as an ultimate value appeals to the unique structure of the alternative of life or death, whereas the link she forges between moral values and the value of life depends on her view of the role of consciousness in our survival. Although Rand grounds reasons for action and moral obligations on the choice to live (to value one's life), denying that this choice is subject to deliberation, she locates nondeliberative grounds for the choice to live in the possibility of directly experiencing one's life as a value. She relies on these same grounds in condemning Taggart and others who reject life. Life, for Rand, is a rational ultimate end in two complementary senses: the choice to value one's life is a rational response to the experience of one's life as a value, and it is only for the sake of life that one needs other values at all.

The Choice to Value

(1990)

ALLAN GOTTHELF

This paper was written for the December 1990 Ayn Rand Society program on the relation of value, obligation, and choice in Ayn Rand's ethics, as a response to Douglas B. Rasmussen's lead paper, "Rand on Obligation and Value." Both papers were read at the meeting and circulated for some years afterwards to ARS members. I have often thought of publishing my paper, especially as it came increasingly to be referred to (and occasionally quoted, with permission) in other people's writings, and I am glad to have the opportunity now. Professor Rasmussen published a revised version of his paper in 2002, with some references to my own; it was reprinted in 2005.

Since my goal is to put on record essentially what I said in 1990, I have for the most part left the paper in the form in which it was circulated. Apart from edits for clarity and a few new footnotes (identified as such), the only changes are those occasioned by Professor Rasmussen's own published revisions. At his request, all quotations from his paper are now cited from the original 2002 published version, and my text has been adjusted in places so that my remarks are now addressed to parallel material in the published version. I do not, however, comment here on any new material in his revised version that did not appear in his original 1990 paper, so the present paper is in no way intended as a response to Professor Rasmussen's post-

1990 work on our topic. Nonetheless, Professor Rasmussen has requested that I provide references to his relevant writings subsequent to his 2002 paper, and I am happy to do so. Likewise, I will refer in the notes to subsequent work, by myself and others, addressing an issue on which I no longer agree with what I said here (or, in one case, usefully amplifying a point I still agree with). But that is all. In short, this paper remains vintage 1990.

The Challenge: Moral Obligation for Ayn Rand Does *Not* Rest on "A Choice to Live"

Is it a principle of Objectivism that all moral obligations are grounded ultimately in a choice to live? In a thought-provoking presentation (and in subsequent writing) Douglas Rasmussen argued no. I will argue yes.

Rasmussen argued as follows. If all moral obligations are grounded ultimately in a choice to live, then the choice to live cannot itself be morally obligated. But if there is no moral obligation to choose to live, then the choice to live is ultimately "optional" or "arbitrary." There would thus be "no reason to be moral," and morality would be "based on an irrational or *a*rational commitment" (2002, 73). On this view, Rand's derivation of "ought" from "is" would apply only to those human beings who have made this "existentialist" or "voluntarist" commitment to morality (2002, 73, 81). The Objectivist morality would then lose the objectivity that many of us think it is Rand's great accomplishment to have established.

As Rasmussen correctly noted, Rand insisted that morality is objective, and vehemently rejected the popular thesis that morality is based on an "irrational or arational commitment." Was her theory of obligation inconsistent with her view that morality is objective? Not at all, Rasmussen proposed, because Rand did not in fact accept the premise of the foregoing argument—the principle that all moral obligations are grounded in the choice to live. On the contrary, he argued, she held that life is an ultimate value for all human beings, whether they have chosen to live or not. Life's status as an ultimate value in no way depends on any choice. It rests, rather, on life's metaphysical nature. The conditional character of life—all life—makes each human life metaphysically an ultimate value for the human being whose life it is, apart from any choices that human beings might make (2002, 74–78).

Rasmussen offered several interconnected arguments for this interpretation of the Objectivist position.

(i) He cited the well-known passage from Rand's essay, "The Objectivist Ethics," in which she presents her definition of an "ultimate value" and explains why life and only life can satisfy that definition (*VOS* 17–18). There is no reference to choice in that passage (2002, 76). (ii) He invoked from Aristotelian studies the concept of an "inclusive end" to show his interpretation compatible with the claim in Objectivist literature that Rand does not "regard any particular value as a metaphysical given, as pre-existing in man or in the universe" (2002, 76 with n7). (iii) He also cited passages from "The Objectivist Ethics" to support his claim that "choices are judged in terms of the end and standard of life" (2002, 77), and not the end of life by any choices.

We must therefore, he inferred, reject the principle under discussion and its consequences. The choice to live does not ground moral evaluation, and so can itself be morally evaluated. "We can even say that a person ought to choose to live" (2002, 78). And we need not ascribe that rejected principle to Rand herself, based on anything she says in her essay "Causality versus Duty," since (iv) when she says there of a human being that "[i]f he does not choose to live, nature will take its course," the most reasonable interpretation is not that she is claiming that failing to choose to live puts one outside the realm of moral evaluation; rather, she is (I infer Rasmussen to be saying) simply noting a consequence of the conditional character of life, the very fact about life that makes it an ultimate value quite apart from any choice any human being might make.[1]

It would seem then, Rasmussen concluded, that Rand rejected the principle that all moral obligation rests on choice. Man's life is the goal and standard of value, and since the achievement of life depends fundamentally on a choice to live, one has a basic, unchosen obligation to make that choice.

Although, on this interpretation of Objectivism, obligation derives wholly from the fact that there is something that, metaphysically, is an ultimate value, one should not infer, Rasmussen observed, that Rand's theory of obligation is a species of consequentialism. The fact that her moral principles take the form of virtues suggests that that conclusion may not follow. So the classification of her theory of obligation must await further discussion (Rasmussen 2002, 80);[2] what is clear, however, is that accord-

---

1. My 1990 paper was, of course, restricted to the arguments then on the table. Rasmussen has offered additional argumentation in his subsequent papers.

2. For my own view of this, see the last section of this paper.

ing to her, fundamental moral obligations derive from the existence of something that is inherently an end in itself, and not in any way from choice.[3]

The Response: Moral Obligation for Rand *Does* Rest on a "Choice to Live"

As I said at the beginning, I believe this interpretation is not correct. I would like to argue (i) that in the Objectivist ethics, all moral obligations are grounded in a choice to live; (ii) that only if there is such a choice to live can Rand's thesis that "[m]etaphysically, *life* is the only phenomenon that is an end in itself" have moral implications for man; and (iii) that this aspect of the Objectivist theory renders the acceptance of morality neither optional nor arbitrary nor irrational nor arational in any proper sense of these terms. In the course of these arguments I will make some observations about the concept of a "basic choice to live," as I understand that concept (and phenomenon), which may help to resolve some of the puzzles surrounding the issues in question.

I think the place to begin is with the prima facie implausibility that Rand would have endorsed the proposition that we have a fundamental moral obligation to live apart from any choice. Consider the following passages from Galt's speech, in *Atlas Shrugged*:

> If I were to speak your kind of language, I would say that man's only moral commandment is: Thou shalt think. But a "moral commandment" is a contradiction in terms. The moral is the chosen, not the forced; the understood, not the obeyed. The moral is the rational, and reason accepts no commandments. (*Atlas* 1018 [*FTNI* 142]).

In saying that "the moral is the chosen, not the forced," Rand is not merely endorsing free will: a duty ethics does not entail determinism. She is rejecting the view that there can be anything one must or should do apart from some basic choice. That basic choice is, of course, the choice to live. Now, consider how that choice, and the moral requirements that follow from it, are characterized in the following passage, from a few pages earlier in the speech:

3. *Note added in 2010*: Professor Rasmussen reports that he has developed and defended his view on the topic in question in three subsequent writings (Rasmussen 2006, 2007a, 2007b), and that these articles contain references to parallel (or otherwise relevant) discussions in published writings by others.

No, you do not have to live; it is your basic act of choice; but if you choose to live, you must live as a man—by the work and the judgment of your mind.

No, you do not have to live as a man; it is an act of moral choice. But you cannot live as anything else— . . .

No, you do not have to think; it is an act of moral choice. (*Atlas* 1015 [*FTNI* 138])

Notice that the two choices that follow in order from the choice to live are each described as moral choices; the choice to live is not. The choice to live is the basic choice that requires a specific mode of action, given the fact that the requirements of man's life, like those of any kind of living thing, are specific. That choice and that fact make all subsequent choices moral choices, as the passage from Galt's speech with which Rasmussen began makes clear:

My morality, the morality of reason, is contained in a single axiom: existence exists—and in a single choice: to live. The rest proceeds from these. (*Atlas* 1018 [*FTNI* 142])[4]

All this, and more, suggests on its face that, in Rand's view, a choice to live antecedes the application of morality to a human being. If one does not accept this interpretation and seeks for some less obvious readings of these passages in order to avoid it, that is because, like Rasmussen, one does not see how such a view is consistent with Rand's discussion of the objective nature of value, and thinks instead that it makes morality radically subjective. These are two distinct points, and we will need to consider them separately.

I start with the well-known passage in "The Objectivist Ethics" where Rand presents her definition of an "ultimate value" and explains why life and only life can satisfy that definition:

An *ultimate* value is that final goal or end to which all lesser goals are the means—and it sets the standard by which all lesser goals are *evaluated*. An organism's life is its *standard of value*: that which furthers its life is the *good*, that which threatens it is the *evil*.

Without an ultimate goal or end, there can be no lesser goals or

---

4. These lines, in fact, follow immediately upon the first of the three passages I have quoted, and their conjunction confirms my interpretation of the first and third passages.

means: a series of means going off into an infinite progression toward a nonexistent end is a metaphysical and epistemological impossibility. It is only an ultimate goal, an *end in itself*, that makes the existence of values possible. Metaphysically, *life* is the only phenomenon that is an end in itself: a value gained and kept by a constant process of action. (*VOS* 17–18)

Rand certainly does not mention choice here (or in the passage's immediate context), and one might maintain that her argument excludes it, since life is said to be metaphysically an end in itself.

But I disagree that her argument excludes it. I suggest that everything said in that passage applies to a human being only if he chooses to live. This condition is necessary because, according to Rand, man, alone of living things, has free will. Plants and nonhuman animals act automatically to further their lives—for them, life is automatically an end in itself, given the nature of life (and the concept of an "end in itself"). Not so for man. A human being does not pursue his survival automatically. A human being must choose to act, he must choose to value, he must choose to seek the continuation of his existence. It is only in the context of this basic choice to continue his existence that man pursues values at all, and only in the context of such a pursuit that one can speak of anything as being of ultimate value to him. Rand's well-known argument that value depends on life shows that *if* a human being chooses to live, then, given the nature of life, his own life is—and only his own life can rationally be—his ultimate value. It is just as true for man as it is for plants and animals, that "[m]etaphysically, life is the only phenomenon that is an end in itself," but it *is* an end in itself for man only so long as it is an *end*—i.e., only so long as it is chosen at all. If it is not chosen at all—if a human being shuts down and stops acting completely—then he has no ends, and no end in itself, and so no ultimate value. And if in Objectivism obligations derive from values, as Rasmussen correctly insists, such a person has no obligations either. He is completely outside the moral realm.[5]

In insisting that moral obligations are grounded in a choice to live, then, I am not disagreeing with Rasmussen that our obligations derive from that which is of ultimate value to us. For I think—and I believe Rand held—that obligations are grounded in the choice to live precisely

5. If he acts again, he reenters the moral realm—although I would argue on psychological grounds that if he does act again, he had not completely renounced the value of life in the first place, and stands condemned for his refusal to pursue that value; but the philosophical point remains. Likewise, although most human beings have limited incentive to shut down completely—to turn their mind and action off completely—continuation remains a choice.

because the status of a human being's own life as his ultimate value is also so grounded. Note that I am not saying that *anything* can become an ultimate value simply by being chosen as such. Like Rasmussen, I insist that only life can be an ultimate value; what I add is that it can be so for a human being only so long as he chooses to continue to exist.

Perhaps "grounded" is the wrong word, and has generated some confusion. Rasmussen asked: "Is life a value because we choose it, or do we choose life because it is a value?" (2002, 75) Strictly, I would say, the answer is neither. Since a value is "that which one acts to gain and/or keep," nothing can be a value to someone apart from his having chosen it. (I'll return to this point in a moment.) But it does not follow from this that life is a value (and an ultimate value) merely because we choose it—as if, were we to choose something else, that new thing would become our ultimate value. The whole point of Rand's derivation of "ought" from "is," as it applies to a human being, is that *if* you choose to exist, *then* you can consistently pursue that choice, and any other particular choice, only by holding your life as your ultimate value since life, by its nature, requires a specific course of action. Only that fact about life gives point to any act of evaluation, gives any reason to choose, gives any basis for a concept of value. But that fact about life has no implication for action to beings who choose not to exist. The choice to live and the nature of life together ground the status of one's life as one's actual, and only rational, ultimate value. That is why, I take it, Rand does not say that her morality is contained in a single choice but "in a single axiom . . . *and* a single choice" (my emphasis).

If one does not accept this interpretation, and insists that life's status as an ultimate value is grounded *only* in its conditional character, one has, it seems to me, only two interpretative directions, neither acceptable as an interpretation of Ayn Rand (and neither philosophically sound). One could claim that life is an ultimate value for man because he is psychologically determined to pursue it. That would allow one to accept Rand's definition of "value" at face value (so to speak): life is in fact something which one acts to gain and/or keep regardless of choice, and it is pursued for itself, regardless of choice. That is surely unacceptable, given everything Rand has said about choice and free will. Or, one could hold that a human being's life is somehow inherently an ultimate value for him, regardless of whether he pursues it or not. And I don't see how one can claim that, without giving life the sort of *intrinsic* value that Rasmussen agrees Rand rejects (2002, 76). That is to say, either every human being aims at life, whether he knows it or not—a thesis I believe Rand would reject, even if a Socrates would not—or life has ultimate value for man wholly independently of whether it is aimed at or not, which makes value an inherent or intrinsic property of life, and not a relationship between life and the conscious, living entity that the human being in question is.

Rasmussen was sensitive to this objection, and sought to reply to it (2002, 76). He quoted an observation made by Nathaniel Branden in *Who Is Ayn Rand?* (1962).[6] Branden had cited a distinction of Leonard Peikoff's between two sorts of intrinsicist theory in order to distinguish the Objectivist theory of value from them both. Branden observed that "in no sense does Ayn Rand regard any particular value as a metaphysical given, as pre-existing in man or in the universe" (Branden 1962, 28). Rasmussen seemed to accept, as I do, that his own account regards the value of life "as a metaphysical given, as pre-existing in man or in the universe," for he replies only that life is not a *"particular* value." Drawing an idea from Aristotelian studies, he argued that life is an *"inclusive* end," and thus not a particular one. Now, while I think there is much to be said for viewing life as an inclusive end in the sense in which that term is used in Aristotelian scholarship, I also think there are important differences between the views of Aristotle and Rand on the relationship of life to its subsidiary ends, which bear on how "particular" the value of life should be viewed.[7] We can sidestep this issue, however, since it seems clear from the context of Branden's discussion that he was using the term "particular" merely as an intensive, and not to divide values into two categories, "particular" and "nonparticular." But one sort of theory being rejected was "conatus" theories, and the things "conated" were as general as "life" or "happiness" (Branden 1962, 28). That being so, then, by Rasmussen's own admission, his interpretation of Rand's theory of value is subject to a description she expressly rejected.

On the interpretation I am defending, however, life possesses value because it is the sort of thing that requires action on the part of its possessor, if it, and its possessor, are to continue to exist, and because the possessor aims at continued existence. If the possessor aimed at continued existence, but that existence did not require any course of action (as

6. The philosophic content of this book was endorsed by Rand as fully consonant with her philosophy (cf. "A Message to my Readers," *TO*, May 1968).

7. *Added in 2010*: I have touched on this issue in Gotthelf 2000, 83; there is now a fuller discussion in Gotthelf 2011.

in the case of the "immortal, indestructible robot" of Rand's "The Objectivist Ethics" [*VOS* 16]), its continued existence (no longer designatable as "life") could not be of value to it. But, likewise, if an entity's continued existence required a specific course of action on the part of its possessor, but its possessor did not, qua the sort of thing it is, in any way aim at continued existence, its continued existence could not be of value to it—nothing could. It is the actual aiming at continued existence, provided automatically in plants and animals, and by volition in humans, that provides the "pole," so to speak, in relation to which, on an objective theory of value, things can be values. Given the conditional character of life, only the actual aiming at continued existence gives living entities the "stake" in life that they need for something to be of value to them; without that stake the conditional character of life is merely a metaphysical fact about them, with no significance for action. That is my view, but I acknowledge that this is a difficult subject worth more discussion.

In my initial summary of Rasmussen's paper I noted three interconnected arguments he gave for his view that the choice to live plays no role in the establishment of life as the ultimate value for man. I've now commented on two of them; on the third I can be brief. All the passages he cited in support of the view that "choices are judged in terms of the end and standard of man's life" (2002, 77) refer to specific choices made in the pursuit of the value of life by those who have already chosen to live. All come from later in "The Objectivist Ethics," after the foundation has been laid and the status of life as an ultimate value has been established.[8] So they do not count against the thesis that the status of life as an ultimate value rests, in part at least, on a basic choice to live.

In addition to these three arguments, Rasmussen offered a reading of the essay, "Causality versus Duty" consistent with his interpretation. He began by asking after the relationship between "choosing not to live" and "not choosing to live" as these terms are used in this context. My own view is this. Since the force of "choosing to live" here is choosing to continue in existence, to think or act at all, and the opposite is simply shutting down, ending all thought, all action, all wish for continued existence, I would propose that there is no effective difference between "choosing not to live" and "not choosing to live." Rasmussen distinguished the two in our con-

---

8. The latter is accomplished in *VOS* 15–16, while the passages Rasmussen cited begin after that.

text, I suspect, because he equated "not choosing to live" with choosing to pursue some value other than life.[9] But the sense of "choosing to live" required by the thesis about moral obligation that I have argued is to be found in Objectivism is the sense I have given it and, given that sense, one cannot equate not choosing to live with choosing something else as one's end. But an adjoining discussion (2002, 73–74) gets the interpretation in question wrong the other way, too: it is no part of the interpretation here presented that the choice to live is implicit in the choice not to live. There is choosing to continue and there is choosing to shut down completely. In choosing to shut down completely, one is *not* choosing to continue.

With all this in mind, let's look at the "Causality versus Duty" passage. Its first paragraph reads: "Life or death is man's only fundamental alternative. To live is his basic act of choice. If he chooses to live, a rational ethics will tell him what principles of action are required to implement his choice. If he does not choose to live, nature will take its course" (*PWNI* 133).

Rasmussen observed that Rand does not explicitly say that if one fails to choose to live (however that is characterized), a rational ethics will *not* tell one the principles of action to follow. That is true. But surely the more natural reading is to take it as implying that. The preceding paragraph announces this paragraph as offering "[t]he proper approach to ethics, the start from a metaphysically clean slate, untainted by any touch of Kantianism" (*PWNI* 133). The slate begins with the fundamental alternative of life or death, and moves directly from this to choice—not to a moral value that requires choice, but to the choice that calls in the realm of moral values. If one chooses to live, the conditional character of life generates ethics; if one does not choose to live (the implication surely is), one does not need nor can one have a code of values; one simply, in due course, goes out of existence. As I observed in regard to other passages from Rand's writings, one would have reason to reject this natural reading only if it had dire consequences. Now, if this reading and the overall interpretation of the Objectivist theory in which it is embedded render the acceptance of morality and the choice to live itself "optional" or "arbitrary" or "irrational"—if they entail that there is no reason to be moral—then their consequences would be dire indeed.

9. That equation seems a premise of the argument in Rasmussen 2002, 78–79, which implicitly generates a large class of people who have "not chosen to live"; see also Rasmussen 2002, 84n10.

Such a Choice (and the Moral Principles Resting on It) as Neither Optional nor Arbitrary

I hold, in fact, that such objections take such terms—"optional," "arbitrary," "irrational," "arational," etc.—out of their normal and proper context, and in doing so confuse two senses of the contrasting term, "necessary."

For it seems to me that to claim that the acceptance of morality is "optional," "arbitrary," an "irrational or arational commitment," and so forth, is to claim that, in a context in which one is *already* existing and acting—in which, in our sense, one has *already* chosen to live—there is no rational basis for action, no reason to act one way rather than another, no facts that make it necessary to act one way rather than another. But, according to the interpretation of Objectivism I have offered, that is false. The very choice to live and act at all, plus the nature of life, gives a person reason—all the reason in the world—to act in a specific way. As Rand herself puts it in "The Objectivist Ethics": "The fact that living entities exist and function [a fact which, in man's case, depends on a basic choice] necessitates the existence of values and of an ultimate value which for any given living entity is its own life" (*VOS* 18).

But what of the choice to live itself? What reason is there to make it? What facts necessitate that choice? What facts make it reasonable to choose to live in the first place? And if none do, isn't that choice, at least, optional or arbitrary? I say no. When one asks what facts necessitate a choice, one can mean only one of two things: what causally necessitates the choice or what morally necessitates the choice. In either sense, the answer from an Objectivist standpoint is "*Nothing* necessitates it." Man has free will, so the basic choice to live is not causally necessitated. And prior to that choice, there is no objective morality. To say that one *should* do X, or that it is *reasonable* to do X, can only mean, on the Objectivist analysis of the concept of value, something like "X is required by one's ultimate value"; but that presupposes that one has an ultimate value. With the choice to live, however, we are speaking of the very choice to have an ultimate value at all—the very choice to value at all. This choice to value is a primary: it is not to be justified by anything prior. Just as, in Objectivist epistemology, axioms are neither proved nor unprovable (in the sense skeptics mean), but are the precondition of proof, so the choice to live is neither reasonable nor unreasonable, but is the precondition for its being reasonable or unreasonable to act in any specific way. But that does not make the choice to live "optional"; the concept simply doesn't apply. Choosing between vanilla and chocolate ice cream is optional: barring unusual factors, one can choose either and be equally moral. More generally, one can isolate three features of the ordinary concept of "optional" that do not apply to the choice to live. First, an optional choice is one that is sanctioned by existing moral principles: one can choose either option and still be moral. This does not apply to the choice to live, since apart from it there *is* no morality. Second, an optional choice standardly is one in which, having chosen whichever option you do, you are present thereafter and able to enjoy the achievement of the option chosen. But the alternative to the choice to live is, in due course, nonexistence; this is an entirely different situation. Third, an optional choice is a choice of the normal, nonbasic (or nonfundamental) type: it is a situation in which you consciously reflect on both options, and if necessary deliberate about them—a situation in which you initiate a process of *evaluation*. But if you do that in the case of a choice to live, if you consciously choose to think about the issue, you are asking its relationship to your already existing ultimate value. Barring the cases of justifiable suicide referred to by Rasmussen, where the ultimate value is actually unachievable (2002, 84), once you ask whether you *should* continue to live, i.e., should take the actions your continued survival requires, there is no option. The only answer, on any reasonable interpretation of Objectivism, is *yes, of course*. Have I reason to take the actions which my continued existence as a rational being requires? Yes, precisely because my continued existence requires them. A basic (or fundamental) choice not to live is not a deliberated choice; it is simply a shutting down. And if it should be the case psychologically that no one reaches that stage without first, across some time, consciously acting against his life (an issue on which I reserve judgment), then it follows that no one can exit the realm of morality guiltlessly. But once he closes down completely, he is, from that point on, as I see it, outside the moral realm.[10]

But let me continue the parallel made in the previous paragraph to metaphysical and epistemological axioms. The choice to live, I am suggesting, is to the realm of values what the axiom of Existence (with its corollary, Identity) is to the realm of knowledge. Each provides the basis

10. *Note added 1995*: This does not, of course, absolve him retroactively of the crime of abandoning the priceless value that is his own life, if indeed the "closing down" was irrational. There are several issues here that need more discussion.

against which things may be judged as rational—rational to accept as true (in the case of the axioms), and rational to value and act for (in the case of the choice to live).[11] But there is a difference. The goal of knowledge is truth, so the axioms can provide the basis they provide only by being *true,* and one needs to explain how they can be known independently of a reasoning process. But moral obligations ("shoulds") are not categorical or intrinsic aspects of reality. Moral obligations *just are* causally necessary requirements of the choice to continue to exist; there is no prior nonconditional truth they must conform to. So there is no such thing as discovering the obligatoriness of the choice to live as there is discovering the truth of a metaphysical or epistemological axiom. There is no realm of intrinsic value to discover and obey. The choice to value is the primary that sets up the realm of values. The nature of life, and of man's life in particular, determines its content. To speak of such a choice as "optional" is to assume the ideal of a nonconditional moral necessity, but that, as Rand has shown, is a contradiction in terms. It is in this context, I think, that Rasmussen in effect confuses two senses of necessity: the optional can be contrasted only with the morally (i.e., the *conditionally*) necessary; something not *unconditionally* necessary is not by that fact alone optional. The basic choice to live, then, is neither morally necessary nor optional.

A Partial Agreement

Let me conclude with a partial agreement. As I noted earlier, Professor Rasmussen observed at the close of his paper that, although for Rand moral obligations derive entirely from ends, the fact that her moral principles take the form of virtues suggests that her theory of obligation may not be a species of consequentialism. I agree. It is certainly not the sort of "act-consequentialism" Rasmussen suggested that it be distinguished from: the basic facts of man's nature and needs are fixed, according to Rand, so that principles are *possible,* and the complexity of concrete situations, the abstractive nature of man's consciousness, and the fact that the harmful consequences of actions are not always perceptually available immediately, are such that principles are *necessary.*[12] Nor, as Rasmussen suggested, is it merely a "rule-consequentialism," since virtues are more

11. *Note added 2010:* This analogy was very nicely elaborated by Irfan Khawaja in his contribution to the December 2000 ARS Book Discussion of Tara Smith's *Viable Values* (Smith 2000), presented at the APA Eastern Division meetings in New York City. Professor Khawaja's paper was subsequently published as Khawaja 2003; see, in particular, 84–87.

12. Cf., e.g., "Philosophy: Who Needs It," *PWNI,* 1–9.

than rules (Rasmussen 2002, 80).[13] I would add one thing. In the typical characterization of consequentialism, one has an end that is an intrinsic good, apart from any choice, and one has the proposition that one is obligated to achieve or maximize that good. Although, as Rasmussen says, the classification of Rand's theory of obligation is for another time, I suggest that we have additional reason to question the classification of her theory with traditional consequentialism, since, as I have argued, her theory of value, and thus obligation, rejects any such notion of an intrinsic good, and rests on a basic choice, in the way I have attempted to describe.[14]

13. Cf. the discussion of this issue as it applies to Aristotle, in the last section of part 1 of Cooper 1975, 76–88.

14. *Added 2010:* In early circulations of this paper, I added references to Peikoff 1991, 241–49, esp. 247–48, and the last section of Binswanger 1992.

As Professor Rasmussen mentioned in the published version of his paper (2002, 80), I reported in the mid-1990s that I no longer agreed with certain statements in this paper. The issues (which I did not there identify) have to do with the nature both of the choice to live and of the refusal to make that choice. (For one thing, there are, for Rand, ways of rejecting life other than completely shutting down [even if such choices do lead ultimately to a complete shutdown, as they do with James Taggert in *Atlas Shrugged*]. Cf., e.g., *Atlas* 1024–25 and 1144–46.) I address these issues in Gotthelf 2011. For discussion that is more in line with my current view, see Darryl Wright's lead essay in the present volume and Salmieri 2011.

METAETHICS
Objectivist
and
Analytic

The Foundations of Ethics
Objectivism and Analytic Philosophy
IRFAN KHAWAJA

nalytic philosophy has been around for more than a century now, and philosophers across its breadth have been engaged in a set of inquiries that go by the name "the foundations of ethics." If one looks at this enterprise historically, or even by reference to the literature of any specific time-period, one finds that "the foundations of ethics" does not ask a single univocal question or define what counts as an answer. It is also rarely clear whether ostensibly competing answers constitute answers to the same question. What one encounters is a proliferation of perspectives, distinctions, and terminology, often very sophisticated, but typically premised on a raft of uncontested stipulations and assumptions. I think it is also safe to say that no one view commands the full allegiance of the discipline (see Darwall, Gibbard, and Railton 1997, 34; Smith 1994, 3–4).

Though (to my knowledge) she did not use the phrase, Ayn Rand formulated the mature Objectivist account of the "foundations of ethics" in the early 1960s, and since then, her views on that subject have occasioned a rather exiguous output of sympathetic commentary—a few books, a few

Thanks to Carrie-Ann Biondi, Paul Bloomfield, Allan Gotthelf, David Kelley, James Lennox, and Michael Young for helpful feedback, both editorial and substantive.

book chapters, a few essays, and a few lectures. If we look at *this* enterprise historically, what we see is in effect the reverse of the picture that obtains in the case of analytic philosophy: here the problem is explicit, but the answer is so compactly expressed that its meaning and significance are unclear. (Indeed, at least one late distinguished philosopher has wondered out loud—to the tune of sixty-four rhetorical questions in eight pages of text—whether the answer really amounts to very much [Nozick 1997; for rebuttal, see Den Uyl and Rasmussen 1981].) But unlike analytic philosophy, there is no real proliferation of perspectives in the Objectivist literature. Objectivists have been saying more or less the same thing about the foundations of ethics since about 1970.

My aim, to clear conceptual space for the Objectivist account of the foundations of ethics for a specifically analytic audience, is very much a metaphilosophical exercise. I am not primarily attempting to rehearse the arguments in defense of the Objectivist ethics as such, but to identify the theory's overarching justificatory structure in such a way as to show (without doing violence to its claims or watering them down) how it is in competition with analytic philosophy on problems that analytic philosophers can recognize as their own. While there is a sense in which the Objectivist account is an answer to a recognizable problem, it offers an original solution that is quite difficult to grasp on the basis of the assumptions of most mainstream analytic philosophy. There is a sense, then, in which the Objectivist account lurks in the "blind spot" of analytic philosophy; in clearing a space for it, I take myself to be identifying this blind spot and explaining why it is one.

Analytic Approaches to the Foundations of Ethics

Given what I've just said about the complexity of the analytic approach to the foundations of ethics, it may help to delimit the field a bit, and also to get a broad overview of the conceptual terrain involved.

In coming to the topic, a first distinction worth making is that between foundationalist and non-foundationalist approaches to the subject. That distinction may at first sound odd, but it marks the very real difference between those whose approach to the foundations of ethics follows from some doctrinal commitment to a version of foundationalism, and those who use the term for rhetorical purposes without intending any such commitment. For purposes of this chapter, I confine discussion of "analytic treatment of the foundations of ethics" to genuine foundationalists and regard "foundations-talk" minus foundationalist commitments to be a rhetorical misnomer.[1]

We then need to distinguish between a commitment to foundationalism that follows from a commitment to epistemic foundationalism, and one that follows from a non-epistemic variety of foundationalism. This distinction will likely be puzzling to many people, and requires some elaboration.

Epistemic foundationalism is one of several theories of justified belief—in other words, theories of the conditions under which a person is justified in holding a belief, and, by implication, of the conditions under which a true belief counts as knowledge (as opposed to, say, being a lucky guess that happens to be true). So construed, foundationalism asserts that an individual's beliefs, when justified, have a hierarchical structure consisting of a foundation and a superstructure. Foundational items confer justification without needing it, and superstructural items are justified insofar as they are asymmetrically supported by the foundation. Borrowing the metaphor of the prototypical house or skyscraper, we have a basement of cognitive items directly in touch with the ground, which supports an edifice of items in indirect contact with the ground via the basement (but only in that way). Understood in this way, foundationalism is a solution to the canonical regress problem first articulated in Aristotle's *Posterior Analytics* I.3, and is a rival, in analytic terminology, of skepticism, infinitism, coherentism, and contextualism.

In one sense, epistemic foundationalism provides an obvious, if not the most obvious, approach to the foundations of ethics in the analytic literature. Suppose that justified belief has the two-tiered structure characteristic of epistemic foundationalism. Suppose further that we *have* some justified moral beliefs. In that case, epistemic foundationalism implies that our justified moral beliefs are either foundational or superstructural. And so the task of giving an account of the foundations of ethics is "simply" the application of foundationalist epistemic strictures to the case of specifically moral belief—no more and no less. Either justified moral beliefs are foundational or they are superstructural or perhaps they are both. The questions are where they go in the structure and why they go there. By common consensus, foundationalism as a general epistemologi-

1. There are borderline cases, e.g., uses of "foundations" metaphors that seem to straddle the line between involving a full-blooded commitment to foundationalist doctrine and being merely casual. See, e.g., Bloomfield 2001, 18, 19.

cal position is thought to entail intuitionism as a moral epistemology, in-tuitionism being the view that regresses of justification involving ethical beliefs terminate with a special class of basic ethical beliefs called "intu-itions," which give us direct access to moral facts, states of affairs, and propositions.

There is, however, another self-consciously foundationalist ap-proach to the foundations of ethics that doesn't take its bearings from foundationalist epistemology. This approach is difficult to describe with precision, in part because there are fewer exponents of this view, and in part because it is unclear what non-epistemic conception of justification is at work here. Nonetheless, one finds notable instances of it in the lit-erature, and these instances are self-consciously foundationalist but self-consciously distinct from the epistemic approach just described, and often self-consciously inspired by the example of specific historical philos-ophers, for example, Aristotle and Kant (see, e.g., Donagan 1977, chap. 7; Gewirth 1978, chaps. 1–3; Gewirth 1984, 192–97; Schneewind 1983, 113–26; MacIntyre 1990; Kagan 1992, 223–42). Its exponents reject the idea that ethics is "just" applied epistemology, and specifically reject epistemic foundationalism and/or intuitionism as viable approaches to ethics. For lack of a better term, call this metaethical foundationalism.

As far as metaethical foundationalism is concerned, the topic of the foundations of ethics is motivated by some variant of the (admittedly vague) question, "Why should I be moral?" A foundationalist theory is one that aims to answer that question head-on. The foundation of the the-ory is the answer to it, and takes the form of a basic moral proposition or prescription.[2] The superstructure of the theory consists, in turn, of a set of principles asymmetrically generated from this basis.

This sort of view comes in two varieties. The resolutely anti-epistemic variety asserts that the "Why should I be moral?" question can be an-swered by a method peculiar to ethics without our having to broach ques-tions in epistemology at all. One inspiration for this view is Aristotle's discussion of practical truth and the practical syllogism at *Nicomachean*

---

2. Though this is not the way it is typically stated, we can, in principle, state the point in the text in terms (not of propositions, but) of *concepts*. A foundationalist ethical theory is one that takes a concept or set of concepts as primitive or basic, and others as asymmetrically de-rivative of or dependent on the basic concepts, where the basic concepts are foundational and the derivative concepts are superstructural. From here it follows that propositions involv-ing only the basic concepts are foundational, and propositions involving derivative concepts are superstructural. See, e.g., Scanlon 1998, 17: "I will take the idea of a reason as primitive." Thanks to Michael Young for helpful discussion of this issue.

Ethics VI.2. Central to this view is the idea that there is a sui generis brand of "practical truth" that differs from theoretical truth and thus involves a different conception of justification than operates in non-practical (i.e., epistemic) contexts. Further, since the conclusion of a practical syllogism is an action rather than a belief, practical justification concerns itself with a different justificandum from what operates in non-practical contexts. Another inspiration is Kant's *Groundwork*. The basic test for the "validity" of a moral claim on Kant's view is universalization of the maxim of the claim, and universalizability is a specifically ethical, not epistemic notion. I confess to finding views of this sort somewhat opaque, but however they are understood, the point is that both views eschew epistemic commitments in favor of "practical" ones.[3]

Another variety of metaethical foundationalism, though hospitable to epistemic commitments, is resolutely antifoundationalist about epistemology, and so combines an attempt to answer the "Why should I be moral?" question with a coherentist epistemology, namely, the method of reflective equilibrium. This approach proceeds in the following way: We are wondering why we should be moral and searching for the answer. We come to the inquiry, however, with certain "pre-theoretical moral beliefs" that constitute our starting point. We reflect on these beliefs, and discard the ones that "seem thoroughly mistaken or at least dubious enough to justify withholding belief" (Timmons 1999, 236).[4] Now we have a set of considered moral beliefs. We then try to make these beliefs coherent. When we succeed (or approximately succeed), we find ourselves in narrow reflective equilibrium. We then expand our efforts to make that first set of beliefs coherent with well-established assumptions from other areas of inquiry. When we succeed here, we are in wide reflective equilibrium. We then ask another question: what principle accounts for our moral beliefs in wide reflective equilibrium? The answer becomes the foundation of ethics, and the set of considered first-order moral beliefs in wide reflective equilibrium becomes their superstructure.

3. For an Aristotelian version of the view, see MacIntyre 2006. For a Kantian version, see Korsgaard 1996b.

4. Though not explicitly a reflective equilibrium theorist, Paul Bloomfield's account of the "ontic foundations" of ethics involves a commitment to something *like* reflective equilibrium without officially endorsing it (Bloomfield 2001). See, e.g., his claim that "altruism has an obvious place in moral theory" (29) and that "it will still be agreed all around that deserting friends and comrades in the midst of battle because of fear is cowardly" (41). These claims function, in effect, as self-justified constraints on the content of morality of the sort officially ratified by reflective equilibrium theory.

One last ambiguity about metaethical foundationalism is worth noting. The subject matter of analytic epistemology is typically the individual epistemic agent: a theory of justification is a theory of the conditions under which *S*, an individual, is justified in believing that *p*. When we refer to "foundation" and "superstructure" in this context, we're referring to *levels within an individual's cognitive set*. The subject matter of metaethical foundationalism is somewhat less clear, but there are two plausible (not necessarily exclusive) possibilities here. One is that the subject matter is *the ideal structure of an ethical theory*: ideally, ethical theories should be constructed so as to have a distinct foundation and superstructure, with the foundation answering the "Why be moral?" question, and then generating or supporting a consistent set of moral claims about what to do in what circumstances. "Foundation" and "superstructure" refer in this context to parts of a theory. Another possibility is that the subject matter is the structure of an *individual's ethically justified action,* where the "ethical justification of an action" is not equivalent to (or eliminable in terms of) the epistemic justification of the belief prescribing the action. Here, "foundation" and "superstructure" refer to the hierarchical structure of an individual's values, where "values" are understood as ontologically distinct from beliefs. Having made this distinction for purposes of clarity, however, I'll ignore it from now on as mostly irrelevant to what I have to say.

I cannot, given space limitations, offer a full critique of any one of the approaches I discuss here, much less of all three. What I'll do instead is to call attention to their basic assumptions from an Objectivist perspective, either suggesting the possibility of alternatives to them or indicating what I take to be their salient weaknesses. My aim here is less to offer a detailed rebuttal of any view than to call attention to the assumptions that analytic philosophers take for granted in doing the foundations of ethics, and which obscure from view what Objectivism has to say on the same topics.

Intuitionism

I begin with the epistemic approach, and in particular with intuitionism, widely regarded as the paradigm of a foundationalist moral epistemology. As many other writers have criticized and defended intuitionism in turn, I make no pretense here to offering a comprehensive discussion; I merely want to list and arrange a series of objections to intuitionism so as to bring to the surface the claims at stake between analytic and Objectivist moral epistemologies. The objections to intuitionism fall into two distinct categories. One set concerns the adequacy of intuitionism as a moral epis-temology per se. Another set concerns the validity of the inference from epistemic foundationalism as a general epistemology to intuitionism as a moral epistemology. Consideration of both sets of objections helps us to see what is distinctive to the Objectivist approach.

Intuitions themselves fall into two categories: a priori and a poste-riori. The most obvious objections to a priori intuitions would come from objections to the possibility of a priori knowledge as such: obviously, if there is no such knowledge, there are no such intuitions. At the very least, we need an account and justification of a priori knowledge if a priori intu-itions are to have a chance of playing a role in moral epistemology. Since Objectivism rejects the possibility of a priori knowledge, it rejects the possibility of a priori intuitions (Peikoff 1991, 54).

There are two objections to intuitions that cut across the a priori/a posteriori distinction. One is just the obscurity of the notion, whether employed in ethics or elsewhere: it is not entirely clear what an "intuition" is supposed to *be*. More fundamentally, however, even if we had in hand an account of what intuitions were, it is not clear why we should regard them as epistemic regress-stoppers in the context of the justification of any given ethical proposition. Suppose we are trying to justify the propo-sition that it is (to use Nozick's example) wrong to subject people to forced labor (Nozick 1974, 33–35, 169–74). How is this proposition *justified* by my intuiting it? There seems little difference between such a "justification" and the sheer table-pounding assertion that "forced labor is *wrong*!" The standard Objectivist position holds that intuitionists neither have nor can have a principled, nonfallacious way of distinguishing justification from dogmatic assertion.[5]

Now consider the inference from epistemic foundationalism as a

---

5. For a good critique along these lines, see Smith 2000, 20–28.

Paul Bloomfield rejects intuitionism of the a priori sort espoused by G. E. Moore, H. A. Prichard, and W. D. Ross, espousing instead a posteriori intuitions of the sort associated with the exercise of skills (Bloomfield 2001, 58, 66). It's not entirely clear to me whether Bloom-field is committed to an a posteriori version of intuition*ism*. He describes the epistemology of skills as involving claims of merely prima facie plausibility and involving prior learning (59). But at times, he seems to be suggesting that a posteriori intuitions are justificatory regress-stoppers: to witness the perceptual facts of a brutal murder is immediately to *see* its wrong-ness (67). The latter interpretation is bolstered by Bloomfield's agreement with Prichard's de-fense of intuitionism in "Does Moral Philosophy Rest on a Mistake?" (Prichard 1912, cited in Bloomfield 2001, 67n7). I would agree with the first set of claims and reject the second: I think there is much to be learned about ethics from reflecting on the epistemology of skills, but would argue that we cannot take skill-based intuitions as justificatorily basic.

theory of justified belief to intuitionism as a theory of justified moral belief. We would be forced to make this inference if, but only if, having adopted foundationalism, we found that intuitionism was the only moral epistemology in town. But this inference is hardly an obvious one, and it is worth bringing to the surface the assumptions that facilitate it. There are, as I see it, three such assumptions, all three of which work together to validate the inference and the denial of which makes the inference a non sequitur.

The first assumption is that all epistemic justification is doxastic. In other words, the structure of justified belief consists at the foundations of self-justified beliefs, and at the superstructure of beliefs justified by way of self-justified ones. It follows from this assumption that there is no such thing as a genuinely cognitive item capable of conferring or having justification that is not itself a belief.

The second and related assumption is that the only possible connection between foundation and superstructure is linear inference: S is justified in believing that p because he infers p from q and q is justified. It follows from the preceding two assumptions that justification proceeds from belief to belief by linear inference. The third assumption is that regress-stoppers for specifically moral beliefs must themselves be moral beliefs. The essentially Humean worry at work here is that since we cannot infer an "ought" from an "is," we cannot justify beliefs with moral content from beliefs with nonmoral content.

If we put the three assumptions together, we can see the straightforward route from foundationalism about justified belief to intuitionism about justified moral belief. Suppose that all of S's moral beliefs are justified. Since all cognitive items must be beliefs, S's foundational items are beliefs. Since foundational items are linked to superstructural ones by linear inference, S's moral beliefs are either self-justifying foundational beliefs or beliefs supported by such beliefs. But since only moral beliefs can justify moral beliefs, to be justified, some of S's moral beliefs must be self-justifying foundational beliefs, that is, moral intuitions. These moral intuitions are the justificatory basis of S's morally justified beliefs. And so foundationalism has led us directly to intuitionism.

Bringing the three assumptions into the open allows us to imagine what would invalidate the foundationalist-to-intuitionist inference. Suppose that we negate all three assumptions I've just described. In that case, we get the following propositions:

1. Some justification is nondoxastic.

2. Some justification is noninferential.

3. Not all regress-stoppers for specifically moral beliefs are themselves moral in content.

If foundationalism can be made compatible with any or all of these claims, we open up nonintuitionist possibilities for a foundationalist moral epistemology, as follows: Suppose again that S's moral beliefs are all justified. Then by foundationalist strictures, those beliefs will have to fall *somewhere* within a foundational/superstructural setup, but they may now do so in forms and locations not dictated by intuitionist strictures. This leads to the possibility that S's belief that p may get its ultimate justification by way of a cognitive item that is not a belief, by way of something other than inference, and by way of a cognitive item that is not moral in content. If such a foundationalism can be defended, then intuitionism will not be the only foundationalist game in town.

Analytic Metaethics

Let me now turn to the two metaethical approaches to the foundations of ethics, beginning with the anti-epistemic version and moving to the coherentist. Again, my aim here is not to offer a comprehensive rebuttal, but to draw attention to the fundamental assumptions presupposed by analytic approaches to the subject, but rejected or disputed by Objectivists.

Metaethics without Epistemology

Recall that this view holds that ethical justification has a foundationalist structure of a non-epistemic variety. A preliminary objection to this view is its sheer obscurity, both in classic and in contemporary guise. It is not clear that contemporary defenders of either the Aristotelian or the Kantian version of this idea have made clear what they had in mind in referring to a non-epistemic form of ethical justification, much less whether they have succeeded in justifying morality that way. That implies, I think, that little progress can be made discussing this view in abstraction from discussions of specific versions of it. Specific versions of the Kantian project have, in my view, successfully been refuted (e.g., Gewirth 1978; Korsgaard 1996b).[6] We could perhaps profit from further discussion of the Aristotelian variety.

---

6. See, e.g., Bernard Williams's refutation of Gewirth in Williams 1985, chap. 4. I discuss Korsgaard's views at length in Khawaja 2008, chaps. 7–8.

A separate problem is that the practitioners of this approach habitually beg the question by front-loading the answers they want into the questions they ask. In this respect, the "Why should I be moral?" question is susceptible to front-loading in two distinct but equally problematic respects. The first is that we can ask the question by presupposing that morality has a fixed content that is not itself being put into question by the question. For instance, if we assume that altruism is an inherent feature of morality, the question "Why should I be moral?" supposes from the start that egoism cannot provide the answer. The second is that we can ask the question by presupposing that a morality (with fixed content) has overriding authority. In this case, the question "Why should I be moral?" supposes that we all should be moral, and merely wonders how we are to convince "the skeptic" of this obvious and antecedently known fact (Smith 2000, 13–19; Khawaja 2008, chaps. 4–5, chap. 7).

If we combine these assumptions, we get an approach to the foundations of ethics that gives only the surface appearance of asking a genuine question and offers only a superficial attempt at justification. On this view, the question "Why should I be moral?" is just elliptical for: "Given that we all know that we ought to be moral, and given that we all know what morality requires, what is the best way of presenting our knowledge so as to refute the moral skeptic?" Asked why these "givens" are givens, one is frequently given one of two answers: either the "givens" just *are* givens, or they are constitutive of the very concept of morality. But either these latter two answers collapse into intuitionism, or they beg the question, or both (for further discussion, see Smith 2000, 13–19).

Metaethics and Reflective Equilibrium

Another approach combines the metaethics just described with reflective equilibrium. Obviously, to the extent that this approach resembles that described as "metaethics without epistemology," the objections that applied there will apply here. But reflective equilibrium, as I see it, creates additional problems that compound the preceding ones.

One problem with reflective equilibrium concerns the "pretheoretical beliefs" with which we supposedly come to moral inquiry. Why should we think that these beliefs have initial probative value? As far as I can see, the answers to this question literally involve ratcheting epistemic standards so far down that the sheer existence of a moral belief amounts, by that fact alone, to the belief's having probative value (see Rawls 1999b, 42–46; Daniels 1976, 264–67; Brink 1989, 123, 134–35; Long 2000, 22–23,

25–27, 52–55; also Timmons 1999, 239–43).[7] But I think it is obvious that the sheer existence of a belief does not by itself confer probative value on the belief any more than wishing for something makes it so.

Nor does it help to be told that the belief has to survive "consideration" or "reflection." For one thing, the standards of reflection in question— what Rawls calls "the characteristics of a competent moral judge"—are too weak and indeterminate to do much work (Rawls 1999a, 2–5). Further, the characteristics are themselves regulable by the considered beliefs they are supposed to be regulating: my conception of "the characteristics of a competent moral judge" is, after all, dependent on my pretheoretical beliefs about morality. If so, those characteristics scarcely furnish a restriction on what I believe: if I believe that *p*, and *p* has probative value simply because I believe it, *p* may well determine what *counts* as "the character of a competent moral judge." For any conflict between my belief that *p* and some conception of these characteristics that conflict with my holding *p*, I need merely redefine the characteristics so that they cohere better with my belief that *p*. I can thereby render "the criteria for moral competence" effectively toothless. The criteria are also (despite contrary protestations) circular: the criteria of the competent moral judge are moral criteria that presuppose the conception of morality that the exponent of reflective equilibrium is trying to justify. But they are also presupposed for purposes of the justification. So the procedure begs the question.

Finally, it cannot be said enough that there is no reason to think that the method of reflective equilibrium tracks moral truth (see Kelley 1986, chap. 6; Haack 1995, chap. 3).[8] Reflective equilibrium is a species of co-

7. Like many authors in this tradition, Daniels (1976) claims that the revisability of the considered moral judgments immunizes reflective equilibrium from the objection made in the text. But revisability is irrelevant to the issue: the question is why considered moral judgments have any probative value *at all*, not whether they can be revised in light of later concerns.

Likewise, Brink (1989) and Long (2000) argue that considered judgments' lack of probative value can somehow be remedied by the adoption of second-order realist beliefs about our capacities as truth-trackers. But this move obviously begs the question: we could only adopt second-order realist beliefs about our cognitive capacities if we had reason to believe that our considered first-order judgments actually tracked the truth. But that is precisely the claim at issue.

8. Norman Daniels concedes that wide reflective equilibrium is insufficient for truth, then says that it "embodies coherence constraints on theory acceptance or justification, not on truth," then doubles back to assert that a "souped up" wide equilibrium is "perhaps" constitutive of truth on an internal realist interpretation in Putnam's sense, but suggests that he is not "inclined" to take the latter route (1976, 276–78). Toward the end of the paper, he offers a series of "highly tentative and programmatic" (and, to my mind, unconvincing and ulti-

herence, but whereas coherence is a relation between beliefs, truth is a relation between beliefs and an independent world. Obviously, since coherence is insufficient for truth, reflective equilibrium is insufficient for truth. But since coherence is not plausibly truth-conducive, neither is reflective equilibrium. Beyond this, since coherence fails to make adequate provision for input from the world, a coherent belief-set is, in principle, compatible with an entirely false one. So the insufficiency of reflective equilibrium for truth is drastic: there is no reason to think that a coherent account of morality is, qua coherent, true.

The preceding is, admittedly, a compressed account of analytic approaches to the foundations of ethics, and I make no pretense of having done justice to the full complexity or power of every conceivable approach. But what I've said is enough to highlight what I previously called analytic philosophy's "blind spot" on the subject, that is, the set of assumptions that obscures the logical space that Objectivism occupies. In particular, what it misses is the possibility of a nonintuitionist, noncoherentist moral epistemology, and a noncircular answer to the "Why be moral?" question.

Terminological Issues

I mentioned at the outset that Ayn Rand never used the phrase "foundations of ethics." For that matter, she neither used the phrase "epistemic foundationalism" nor discussed epistemology in a way that analytic philosophers would find recognizable. One might wonder, then, both from an analytic perspective as well as from an Objectivist one, about the propriety of discussing her views in a terminology foreign to her own. Rand had strict methodological scruples about philosophical terminology and was suspicious to the point of contempt of analytic philosophical jargon. For one thing, she formulated what she called "Rand's Razor," which tells us never to multiply concepts beyond necessity or integrate them in disregard of it (*ITOE* 72). For another, she often suggested that contemporary philosophers have neglected fundamental philosophical issues by getting lost in pseudodebates generated by false dichotomies and word games.

---

mately inconclusive) speculations about the relations among coherence, convergence, objectivity, and truth. But his official view is that questions about the relation between coherence and truth are "an *idle* worry in the absence of any specific research capable of destabilizing the equilibrium" (1976, 278; emphasis in original). This latter claim surely gets methodological priorities wrong: why would we have reason to embark on "specific research" by way of reflective equilibrium unless we had reason to think it truth-conducive? In any case, ethical egoism is precisely a case of "specific research capable of destabilizing the equilibrium."

As Leonard Peikoff (1991, 141) states, "When thinkers base their theories not on the facts of reality, but on the unscrutinized conclusions of their predecessors, the result is a uniquely repellent kind of intellectual structure—not a hierarchy of knowledge, but of increasingly contorted and insolvable errors."[9]

Though I have sympathy with these criticisms as applied to many other philosophical issues, I do not think they apply in the present case. The term "foundationalism" is, to be sure, a piece of specifically analytic jargon, but while Rand doesn't use that precise word, both she and Peikoff make constant reference in epistemic contexts to the notion of a foundation, use the same architectural metaphor that analytic philosophers use to illustrate it, and allude to versions of the regress argument in order to motivate it (Peikoff 1991, 120; VOS 17–18). Further, Peikoff's discussions (1991, 116) of the nature of objectivity, though formulated in a terminology that would be alien to analytic epistemologists, is nonetheless explicitly on the very topic at the center of analytic epistemology—the relationship between knowledge and justification.

Neither Rand nor Peikoff use the phrase "foundations of ethics," either. But Rand opens her discussion of the Objectivist ethics by describing the task of ethics as follows: "The first question that has to be answered, as a precondition of any attempt to define, to judge, or to accept any specific system of ethics, is: Why does man need a code of values?" (VOS 13–14). This passage by itself suggests that an ideal ethical theory takes a foundational-superstructural form: the answer to the "first question" is the foundation, and the specification of the rest of the system is the superstructure. Later in the same essay, Rand offers a regress argument to answer her "first question" (16–18), explicitly rejecting in her own terminology what analytic philosophers would call skepticism (15), as well as contextualism (15–16), coherentism (16), and infinitism (17–18) as candidate answers to it. She criticizes Aristotle, in effect, for being insufficiently foundationalist in his approach to ethics (14). According to Rand, Aristotle describes the virtuous man and virtue itself but does not tell us what it is about the world that requires us to engage in goal-directed action in the first place. The latter criticism amounts to saying that while Aristotle offers an account of virtuous action by way of the regress argument at *Nicomachean Ethics* I.1–2, he stops the regress prematurely in the

---

9. Following Allan Gotthelf (2000), I take Peikoff's book to be a "quasi-primary source" for Rand's thought (25–26), but take the "quasi-" to imply defeasibility as to the correct interpretation of the Objectivist position. See note for a significant disagreement.

function argument of *Nicomachean Ethics* I.7, relying too heavily there on coherence with common belief to make his case.

I think, then, that it does no violence to Rand's theory to call it a form of foundationalism, provided that we define foundationalism very broadly.[10] A theory counts as foundationalist so long as it: (a) is a theory of justification that purports to answer a regress argument; (b) is incompatible with skeptical, coherentist, contextualist, and infinitist answers to the regress; (c) identifies a foundation of items that ends the regress; and (d) derives a superstructure from this foundation. By this definition, Rand is a foundationalist both about epistemology and about ethics and has something to say about the relationship between those two commitments.

Objectivist Moral Epistemology

In summary, the Objectivist epistemology says something like this: as with varieties of analytic foundationalism, we have a regress argument that requires us to divide cognitive items into the foundational and the superstructural. At the foundations, we have sensory perception, understood on a direct realist model. Rand defines "perception" as "a group of sensations automatically retained and integrated by the brain of a living organism, which gives it the ability to be aware, not of single stimuli, but of entities, of things" (*VOS* 20). So understood, perception gives us direct, noninferential, nondoxastic contact with objects and properties in the world, including the similarities and differences between those objects. Crucially, Rand takes perception to exhaust foundational items: there are, on her view, no foundational *beliefs*. All of our beliefs, then, are in the superstructure, asymmetrically supported by perceptions in the foundation. Obviously, the preceding applies to moral belief, as well. If we assume ex hypothesi that we have justified moral beliefs, those beliefs will be justified, ultimately, by the evidence of the senses.

10. Many previous commentators have described Objectivism as foundationalist, and interestingly, these commentators follow the same rough pattern as the one I described in analytic philosophy. David Kelley describes the Objectivist epistemology as foundationalist but does not specifically discuss its moral epistemology; see Kelley 1986, 218–28, and Kelley 1991, 165–79.

Tara Smith (2006, chap. 2), Allan Gotthelf (2000, chap. 9), Harry Binswanger (1992, 84–104), and Douglas Den Uyl and Douglas Rasmussen (1986, 63–69) discuss Rand's account of the foundations of ethics but do not explicitly tie this commitment to her epistemology.

Two exceptions to this general rule are Long 2000, and Machan, 1982, 23–49, both of which discuss both epistemology and ethics. But Long's views are obviously at odds with mine, and Machan pursues slightly different issues than I do.

So we have perception at the foundational level and belief at the superstructural. But while perception exhausts the foundational level, belief does not exhaust the superstructural. On Rand's view, the link between perception and belief is supplied by concepts. A concept is "a mental integration of two or more perceptual concretes, which are isolated by a process of abstraction and united by means of a specific definition" (*VOS* 21). Abstraction, in turn, is "the power of selective focus and treatment; it is the power to separate mentally and make cognitive use of an aspect of reality that cannot exist separately" (Peikoff 1991, 78).

The general idea is that while the perceptual level is the "given," human beings have the cognitive power to abstract from the perceptual level and form concepts that condense our perceptual information in cognitively useful ways. Though these concepts are all on the superstructural side of the foundation-superstructure divide, they differ in their *distance* from the perceptual level. At the first level, we have concepts of objects directly accessible in perception (e.g., "table"). At another level, we have concepts formed by abstraction from the first level (e.g., "furniture"). At another level, we have concepts formed by abstraction from the second level (e.g., "antique")—and so on. Concepts differ, as well, in *content*. And so there are concepts of objects and properties in the world external to consciousness (e.g., "table," "chair," "length," "animal"), those internal to consciousness (e.g., "thought," "feeling," "desire," "pleasure"), and hybrid concepts that include elements of both (e.g., "education," "learning," "theory," "law"). In *ITOE*, Rand offers a detailed account of these concepts and how they are formed, and of the hierarchical structures into which networks of concepts fall.

I think it is obvious enough why Rand's theory is foundationalist, and also why it instantiates precisely the structure that constitutes an alternative to intuitionism about moral epistemology: justification on this view is neither restricted to the doxastic nor the inferential, nor are moral beliefs justified by other moral beliefs (or other items with moral content). Everything, ultimately, is justified by the evidence of the senses, construed in non-doxastic and non-inferential terms. So there is no a priori knowledge and no intuition-based regress-stoppers, hence no room for intuitionism.

I need to do some fine-tuning to make some of the Objectivist epistemology's more heterodox claims clear. Three points where it diverges from analytic epistemology are worth making here.

Analytic philosophers consistently distinguish between justified belief and knowledge, and take foundationalism to be a theory of justified belief, not knowledge. By contrast, standard presentations of the Objectivist epistemology present it as a theory of knowledge, making no explicit mention of justified belief. This may seem to imply that analytic and Objectivist epistemologies are about different topics, but that need not be the case.

Suppose that knowledge is something like justified true belief, and suppose that "justification" is a strongly truth-conducive notion. Then, obviously, there is going to be some considerable overlap between the structure of justified belief and that of knowledge: they will be identical in every case where justified belief happens to be true. The stronger the connection between justification and truth, the greater the overlap. I propose, then, that the Objectivist theory be categorized with the family of analytic theories that take "epistemic justification" to be a truth-conducive teleological concept, as many do.[11] Further, while "epistemic justification" is not (always) explicitly discussed under that precise description in the Objectivist literature,[12] the references to objectivity and epistemic responsibility that are discussed there amount in my view to the same thing.

Another difference is a little more substantive. It is a dogma among certain analytic epistemologists that justification is *inherently* inferential and/or that all perception is theory-laden or irreducibly doxastic. Thus many epistemologists *define* foundationalism as a view that requires self-justifying beliefs, thereby excluding an Objectivist-type foundationalism from the menu of options.[13] But this is changing. The Objectivist espousal of direct realist foundationalism, though still a minority view, is no lon-

---

11. See William Alston (1985) for his discussion of what he calls J_e ("having truth-indicative grounds within one's perspective") as well as proposition XXI. See also Kelley 1991.

12. The exception to this rule is Kelley, who *does* use that term; see note 10.

Though I've taken Leonard Peikoff's views as a "quasi-primary" source of Objectivist doctrine, I dissent from his view on the specific issue discussed in this paragraph. Puzzlingly and, to my mind, problematically, Peikoff (1991, 171) asserts that objectivity (i.e., epistemic justification) is always sufficient for knowledge. I see no basis in *ITOE* for this claim and Peikoff offers no evidence that Rand held it. Further, the independent argument he offers for the claim seems to me to raise more questions than it answers (Peikoff 1991, 171–81; a similar criticism appears in Kelley 1991).

Peikoff also asserts that moral virtue can be insufficient for happiness (1991, 327–28). The claim is puzzling in light of Peikoff's avowal of the sufficiency of objectivity for truth. Both moral virtue and epistemic justification are, on the Objectivist view, teleologically related to their ends. It's unclear why Peikoff thinks of the teleological relation as indefeasible in the epistemic case but defeasible in the ethical one.

13. For a typical example, see Plantinga 1993, 73.

ger unheard of. In psychology as well as epistemology, direct realism is finding adherents (e.g., Haack 1995; see also LeMorvan 2004, 221–34). Obviously, then, Objectivism belongs to the family of foundationalisms that allow for the possibility of nondoxastic cognition and noninferential justification.

The following difference is the most important and most complex. Analytic epistemologists take foundationalism to be a theory of justified *belief*, farming talk of concepts out to philosophers of mind or language. By contrast, it is *concepts*, not belief, that are at the center of the Objectivist view. In one sense, this fact might, again, induce one to think that the two theories concern totally different topics. From an analytic perspective, talk of concepts is just out of place in a theory of justification. Justification applies to beliefs, and beliefs are propositional. What does concept-formation have to do with epistemic justification?

It seems to me that this objection is really a consequence or version of the second analytic assumption just discussed. If we give up the idea that foundations must be doxastic, we give up the rationale for the idea that the relation between foundation and superstructure must be inferential. Absent these assumptions, if concepts are not the link between foundations and superstructure, it is not clear what other link would exist. Foundationalists from Descartes to Chisholm have faced the difficulty that the doxastic foundations they have identified—the supposedly "self-justified" beliefs—are too thin to support any minimally robust superstructure of justified belief. There is also the problem that linear inference is a very artificial and oversimplified conception of justification: even the simplest belief is justified by a network of propositions, not by one in isolation. A foundation of self-justifying beliefs cannot account for this, but neither can the attempt to get from the perceptual level directly to beliefs without the help of concepts (Kelley 1986; Haack 1995).

But beliefs can be decomposed into their constituent concepts, and the Objectivist theory gives us an account of how the concepts can be derived from perception. The justificatory relevance of the theory should be obvious: to epistemically justify S's belief that p, we decompose p into its constituent concepts, and ask whether S has, or could in principle, retrace the process by which S formed those concepts. It is at least a necessary condition of S's being justified that S's cognitive processes should match the norms that govern concept-formation for concepts of the relevant kind. Since the norms are norms that link the concept to perception, and perception is a form of cognitive contact with the world, norms of concept-formation tie our concepts (and by implication our beliefs) *to* the world (*ITOE* 27). All of this applies, mutatis mutandis, to moral epistemology. In this connection, Rand lays out norms governing the formation of three sorts of moral concepts—what she calls concepts of "teleological measurement," concepts of "method," and "composite concepts of method" (*ITOE* 32–37).

An interesting implication of Rand's theory of concepts is that it introduces a complexity and richness that is missing from standard analytic accounts of the relation between foundation and superstructure in a foundationalist theory. On the analytic view, foundationalism involves *one* sort of epistemic asymmetry: superstructural beliefs are asymmetrically dependent for their justification on foundational beliefs. On the Objectivist view, foundationalism involves *three* sorts of asymmetry: beliefs depend on perception; concepts depend on perception; and concepts depend on other concepts. Much of this complexity has yet to be worked out, but I think it holds out a great deal of untapped promise for a defensible form of foundationalism, both generally and in moral epistemology.

Objectivist Metaethics

As we have seen, in her explicitly ethical work, Rand takes herself to be asking a version of the "Why be moral?" question, but it is a significantly different version, and I think a better one. Let me continue her discussion of that question from where I previously left it:

> *Why* does man need a code of values?
>
> Let me stress this. The first question is not: What particular code of values should man accept? The first question is: Does man need values at all—and why? (*VOS* 14)

Like "Why be moral?" this is a justificatory question about the status of morality, whose answer functions, metaethically, as the foundation of ethics. Unlike "Why be moral?" however, it makes far fewer presuppositions about morality, and thus has better claim to being an ultimate justificatory question. It does not assume that morality has any specific content—for example, that it requires or excludes egoism or altruism, or that it requires or excludes justice or benevolence, etc. Nor does it assume that moral claims must take some specific form: categorical or conditional, absolute or flexible, universalizable or particularistic. It does not even assume that morality is justifiable: it leaves open the possibility that it is not.

Most fundamentally, it doesn't take for granted that humans are required to take goal-directed action at all.

The question asks what, if anything, requires us to take goal-directed action. Assuming that we answer this question (and only if we do), it asks whether our pursuits must take the form of a "code" or need not—where the term "must" gets its content from the sense of requirement involved in answering the first question. Because the question is fundamental, the answer, if correct, accounts for *more* than is possible to any answer to the "Why be moral?" question or its cognates. And because the question presupposes nothing about morality's form or content, it has a hope of justifying what it says about both in a noncircular way. To the best of my knowledge, no one in the history of philosophy has asked quite this question, given quite Rand's answer, or used the answer to provide the foundation of ethics.[14]

Her answer to the "first question" turns on what she describes as the conditional character of life. As a general biological phenomenon, life is a process of self-sustaining and self-generated action (*VOS* 16). In other words, a living being's very existence depends on its engaging in a complex repertoire of continuous goal-directed action across its lifespan, generated and directed by the organism itself. The nature of the organism determines the kind of action appropriate to its survival. Because each organism has a determinate nature, each has needs, and so each has a determinate mode of life across its lifespan appropriate to its capacities and environment. Given the determinacy of modes of life so conceived, there is such a thing for each type of organism as acting in accordance with and acting against the requirements of life—the most obvious requirements being those of physical health and functionality, the less obvious (for conscious organisms) including proper mental functioning and psychological health. An organism's default on its mode of life undermines or impairs its functionality in proportion to the significance of the default; extreme default undermines its existence altogether, but default of a less severe variety leads to damage or injury.

14. Contrary to both Jack Wheeler (1986, 81) and Roderick Long (2000, 30), I do not think Rand's question corresponds to the question that motivates Aristotle's ethical theorizing: Aristotle takes goal-directed action for granted; he does not seek to explain why we must engage in it.

Korsgaard (1996b) seems to ask something like Rand's question, but conflates it with several others throughout the book, and (consequently) offers an answer at odds with Rand's. I discuss Korsgaard's views at length in Khawaja 2008, chaps. 7–8.

The optimal course of action for an organism is one that most efficaciously promotes survival values while minimizing the probability of harm in every action that the organism takes across its lifespan. The life-promoting, on the Objectivist view, is good for the organism (and the basis for judgments/predications of goodness), the life-subverting, bad (and the basis of the corresponding judgments/predications). I'll call this complex fact the "conditionality of life," the thesis expressing it the "conditionality thesis," and the entities to which it applies, "conditional entities."[15]

Put in this way, the conditionality thesis may sound more like a piece of biology than of metaethics or ethics. Its relevance to ethics becomes clear via an essentialist interpretation of the nature of conditional entities, and the application of this essentialism to the human case.

On Rand's view, life is, for all organisms regardless of complexity, a process of self-sustaining and self-generated action: the capacity for self-generated self-sustenance is the defining feature of the class of organisms. As previously remarked, each type of organism differs fundamentally from every other, and the differences supply the criteria of a science of biological and anthropological systematics. But if we inquire into the capacities of any given organism, we find that we can partition those capacities hierarchically into those most causally responsible for generating and guiding actions, and those that are controlled by and guided by the former group. The generative and guiding capacities are essential, the controlled and guided elements, not-so. (I hasten to add that "not essential" is *not* equivalent to "dispensable" or "unimportant": my point is that the essential capacities preserve the non-essential ones *by* preserving the optimal conditions of their own functioning.) So self-preservation for any organism is principally the promotion of its existence by promoting the optimal conditions for the operation of its *essence* across its natural lifespan. In the case of organisms with consciousness, their unique mode of consciousness is their essential capacity, or as Rand puts it, their "basic means of survival" (*VOS* 19). In the human case, rational agency is the essence. So humans survive principally by using reason to promote the optimal conditions for the operation of rationality across the human lifespan.

That brings us to the application of the conditionality thesis to the human case. On Rand's view, (adult) human beings are rational agents

15. I borrow and slightly modify the preceding two paragraphs from my discussion of Smith 2000, in Khawaja 2003, 71.

who possess libertarian freedom but lack innate knowledge of any action-guiding kind. Thus agents have a power for choice and rationality, but lack an automatic means of generating or guiding their actions. Assume ex hypothesi that an organism of this sort seeks optimal survival. If so, it would have to actualize the (unified set of) capacities that could be expected to sustain its rational agency across its natural lifespan of some seven to ten decades. To do so, it would have to pursue an interconnected set of goals or values. To do that, it would have to partition possible objects of pursuit into two categories: the *ex ante* survival-optimal (hence good) and the *ex ante* nonoptimal (hence not-good). To do *that*, it would need to project the pursuit of the first and the avoidance of the second across its whole lifespan with the aim of grouping the choiceworthy values, as much as possible, as choiceworthy-across-a-whole-lifespan (call these "lifespan interests"), and individuating other choiceworthy values by their contribution to these (call these "derivative interests"). Among the lifespan interests, some would concern the *traits* worth cultivating and the *norms* worth adhering to across a whole lifespan. Call the first "moral virtues" and the second "moral principles."

We can now see how Rand is a foundationalist in the metaethical sense. The result of the full inquiry I have just described would be an egoistic moral theory with a foundation based in the conditionality of life, and a superstructure of virtues and principles defined by their promotion of life. Obviously, a fully worked-out version of this theory would be an extremely complex affair (the two clearest and most comprehensive discussions are Peikoff 1991, chaps. 6–9, and Smith 2006). It would, for a start, require an account of the basic features of rationality (and accompanying moral psychology). It would then have to identify the range of possible traits and norms capable of functioning as lifespan interests and find the compossible set that *best* functioned in that way. It would, finally, have to integrate the preceding facts with an account of human sociality. But the result, when finished, would answer the fundamental question about normativity, would identify an ultimate object of pursuit, and would identify the structure of an ideal theory.

Between Epistemology and Metaethics

I have suggested that the Objectivist approach to the foundations of ethics is foundationalist in two apparently different senses, one epistemic and one metaethical. In the epistemic sense, foundationalist strictures require us to reduce or trace back our beliefs to the perceptual level via the concepts that constitute those beliefs. On this view, we are fully justified in a belief when we trace it back to its foundation in the evidence of the senses. And what is true of beliefs generally is true of moral beliefs as well. In the metaethical sense, we face the task of explaining whether human beings need to value, and if so, whether human beings need a code of values. In this sense, justification consists in generating prescriptions from the requirements of survival qua human, or else checking to see whether putative ethical prescriptions do or do not make a positive contribution to survival as our ultimate end—accepting them if they do and then integrating them into a coherent structure of prescriptions, rejecting them if they do not. It also requires us to theorize in such a way as to keep this latter constraint firmly in mind.

In my experience, analytic philosophers tend to regard these two types of theory as distinct and discrete commitments, and do not much talk about the relations between them (or else actively disavow that any exist). The same thing is true, albeit to a lesser degree, of Objectivist philosophers, who, when it comes to "the foundations of ethics" typically discuss the metaethical rather than epistemic strain of Rand's arguments.[16] But what is the relation between the two types of foundationalism about ethics? Are they two distinct types of foundationalism, or two ways of describing the same one? My (tentative) answer is that on the Objectivist view, the metaethical type of foundationalism turns out to be reducible to the epistemic without being eliminable in favor of it.[17]

Why non-eliminable? Well, suppose ex hypothesi that the conditionality thesis is true. To grasp its truth, as Rand puts it, is "*in part* to retrace the process" by which a rational agent would form the concept "conditionality of life" from the perceptual level, "to grasp at least *some* of the units it subsumes" (*ITOE* 27; my italics in the first case, Rand's in the second). As a model, think of how one might teach the concept to an undergraduate, conveying it by examples perceptually available to the student (e.g., plants, animals, people), and asking the student inductively to generalize from that sample to the world beyond it. Clearly, then, the very process of grasping the meaning of a metaethical concept (or proposition) is a matter of forming the concept in the right way from per-

---

16. Leonard Peikoff is a notable exception. At *OPAR* 207–13, he (correctly) stresses that a defense of the conditionality thesis requires a tracing-back of normative concepts to the evidence of the senses. See also *OPAR* 243 for a restatement of a similar point: "Moral knowledge . . . follows the pattern of all conceptual knowledge."

17. Thanks to Michael Young and David Kelley for helpful conversation on this topic.

ception. So epistemic considerations cannot literally be divorced from metaethical ones.

But notice the phrases "in part" and "at least some" in the passages just quoted. What the passages suggest, I think, is that in first grasping and applying metaethical concepts, we do not and need not begin by engaging in an elaborate, full-bore, microlevel reconstruction of the process of concept-formation from perceptual evidence. We grasp any given concept in an epistemically justified but still preliminary way. It is important to see that we can, at this preliminary level, be genuinely justified in the claims we make about morality. If you ask why you should be moral, I can say that you should be moral because as a conditional entity, your existence and identity depend on being moral: your survival requires the promotion of lifespan interests, and those interests require a determinate mode of goal-directed action. I can say, as well, that virtue is one of those lifespan interests. I can then enumerate the virtues, spell out their requirements, and explain why vice subverts your self-interest. All of this is genuine knowledge, and none of it requires a full-scale reduction to perception in order to count as the sort of knowledge that Aristotle calls *gnosis* (*Nicomachean Ethics* I.4 1095b 1–5). So we can have the "metaethical account" of the foundation of ethics in partial autonomy of the epistemic account, hence the non-eliminability of the metaethical account.

Why is the metaethical type of foundationalism reducible? Again, suppose that the conditionality thesis is true and that we have the kind of metaethical justification I have just described. The metaethical account gives us a serviceable justification of ethical claims even if we do not have a full-scale reduction of the relevant concepts to the perceptual level. But the foundationalist strictures of the epistemology demand a deeper and more ambitious type of justification as well. At this deeper level, it is not sufficient to show that a particular norm or trait promotes survival; what we ultimately need is (not just that) but a full, thorough demonstration of how every concept of every candidate norm is grounded in sensory perception. That is, to be sure, a grand-scale project, but it is, on the Objectivist view, what is required to produce an ethics worthy of the description of *episteme*.[18]

---

18. Peikoff seems to be making a similar point at *OPAR* 120: "'Proof' is the process of establishing truth by reducing a proposition to axioms, i.e., *ultimately*, to sensory evidence" (my italics). The word "ultimately" implies the sort of two-stage justification I describe in the text. See also Peikoff's "caution" about tracing concepts to perception "in essential terms" at first, and only later filling in "further nuances" (*OPAR* 139).

In offering this account of analytic versus Objectivist approaches to the foundations of ethics, I've been operating at a very high level of abstraction, discussing both views in programmatic ways, and leaving out a great deal of detail and fine-grained argumentation. But my aim has been basically structural—to compare and contrast the "architecture" of two approaches to the foundations of ethics.

There is, as my account suggests, quite a lot to be done in order to bear out the promise of the Objectivist theory, as Rand herself implied.[19] At the epistemic level, I can think of three large-scale projects: (1) a theory of the hierarchical structure of concepts; (2) a theory of specifically moral concepts, elaborating on the very brief comments on that subject in chapter 4 of *ITOE*; and (3) a theory of the method by which beliefs are traced to the perceptual level. At the metaethical level, I can think of two projects: (1) a more worked-out notion of "life" as the ultimate value; and (2) a more worked-out method of describing what life requires, both in ethics and in politics.

But there is also, I think, a rather complex and well worked-out structure here—a theory that for all of its heterodoxy, is radical, coherent, and original. The nondoxastic conception of foundationalism and accompanying theory of concepts seem to me a signal advance over the doxastic/ deductive varieties of foundationalism that have reigned in epistemology since Descartes. The conditionality of life as the basis of ethics seems to me a more promising foundation for the virtues than the botanical metaphors that dominate the virtue ethics literature ("flourishing"), and a more promising basis of norms than the principle of utility, the categorical imperative, contractual agreement, divine command, or intrinsic value theory. Finally, the idea that epistemic and metaethical foundationalisms are connected parts of an integrated theory is also something original

19. The claims in this paragraph are deliberately ambiguous between two different interpretations: (1) that the tasks I lay out represent lacunae in *Rand's* theorizing, and (2) that the tasks represent lacunae in *our* understanding of the implicit content of Rand's theorizing. I remain neutral as between these two interpretations. Some of Rand's own claims seem to favor the first interpretation. She describes *ITOE* as "a preview" of a planned (but ultimately unwritten) "future book on Objectivism" (*ITOE* 1), and denies that *VOS* is a "systematic discussion of ethics," referring to it instead as "a series of essays on those ethical subjects which needed clarification, in today's context" (*VOS* xii). Both claims seem to suggest lacunae in her theorizing. But given the existence of the "oral tradition" alluded to by Gotthelf (2000, 2, 25–26), and given the remarkable compression and fertility of her writing, the second interpretation is possible. Thanks to Allan Gotthelf for pressing these issues, though I should emphasize that he does not endorse all the claims I make here.

and important. Without being overly triumphalist, then, I think it is safe to say that analytic philosophy has something to learn from Objectivism.

Perhaps more important than any single thesis or combination of theses is the aspiration behind the Objectivist account of ethics. "A 'moral commandment,'" Rand wrote five decades ago, "is a contradiction in terms. The moral is the chosen, not the forced; the understood, not the obeyed. The moral is the rational, and reason accepts no commandments" (*Atlas* 944). For all of the sophistication and accomplishments of analytic philosophy, it is remarkable how often it has lapsed in its justifications of morality into appeals to force and demands for obedience. One famous contemporary philosopher speaks of bringing "the sanctions of the law and social pressure" against those he cannot persuade of his views about ethics (Singer 1993, 335); another tells us in all seriousness that "folk wisdom" is the "only court of appeal there is for claims about what we have normative reason to do" (Smith 1994, 195–96). A third tells us that "if you can't help believing" in morality's authority, "you'd better believe it." For "in the beginning, and in the end, is the conviction" (Dworkin 1996, 118).

But reason is not so easily cheated. What reason accepts and demands is its own satisfaction: to act on norms it *knows* to be right, and to follow them in the knowledge that they are. Knowledge, as Rand put the point, is the mental grasp of a reality that exists independently of the mental act of grasping it: "man determines the truth or falsehood of his judgments by whether they correspond to or contradict the facts of reality" (*PWNI* 27; cf. *ITOE* 35). If nothing else, what Objectivism demands is that we strain every nerve to meet this standard: to know with certainty that we've made the utmost attempt to know. In the most fundamental sense, this attitude is the precondition for any inquiry into the foundation of ethics, as it is of inquiry as such. Whatever there is to be said about analytic philosophy or Objectivism, we should accept no less from others, and demand no less from ourselves.

Egoism and Eudaimonism
Replies to Khawaja

PAUL BLOOMFIELD

rfan Khawaja has written a provocative chapter on the fundamental aspects of Ayn Rand's moral philosophy, a treatment that he sees as being intimately tied up with her epistemology. There is too much there for me to comment on even most of it. I'll focus here on those aspects of the work about which I think I have something interesting, and perhaps helpful, to say. I should say up front that I am far from being any sort of expert on Rand's philosophy. I am not completely ignorant, but I am sure that I have been asked for my opinion for reasons other than my familiarity with her work; my specialty is analytic metaethics and I write here from that point of view. And while drawing the metaethical/normative distinction is part of the dialectic in the present context, I have a particular side-interest in the normative question of "Why be moral?" and the normative relations between morality and self-interest.

Khawaja has written on the relations between Objectivism and analytic philosophy, and since I am approaching the relations from the other direction, I think a good place to begin is with the dialectical and rhetorical situation. This will, I hope, lead us right into the philosophy.

I see Khawaja's project as drawing together two distinct topics that seem better if kept apart. I think ambiguities of the word "foundations" require disentanglement. Metaethics is the study of the foundations of morality, and "Why be moral?" is a foundational question in morality, arguably the single question that drives moral and ethical philosophy. I think, however, it is best to keep the metaethical questions about the ontology and epistemology of morality separate from directly normative questions about how to live.

The distinction between metaethics and normative ethics is of course explicitly disputed. Ronald Dworkin (1996), Simon Blackburn (1998), and Richard Rorty (1982, introduction) have, for a variety of reasons denied the distinction (for response, especially to Dworkin, see Bloomfield 2009). But since Moore (1993), many scholars have commonly accepted the distinction in mainstream analytic philosophy. At the very least, it seems as if a conference on metaethics is likely to discuss mostly different topics than a conference on normative ethical theory. In any case, if we do hold on to the distinction, I think we should distinguish the topics in Khawaja's paper along the same lines.

There is a lot going on philosophically in Rand's work. In a single essay, like "The Objectivist Ethics" (*VOS*), she can range from issues in normative ethics to epistemology to philosophy of mind, and while Rand most likely had at least a loose picture of how these fit together, I hope to show that we can tease apart some questions from others; the answers to some questions do not bear on the answers to others. It does seem true to say that Rand's central concern was the question "How to live?" and her answer was in the philosophical driver's seat.

Dialectically, Rand's goals were no different from those of most traditional moral philosophers. We all share an interest in how to live well and in what the theoretical basis is for this shared, rough idea of "the good life." These shared starting points and theoretical concerns are in contrast to the rhetorical posture that I think I see in Khawaja's paper, and probably in Rand's work itself, in relation to philosophy as it is typically done in the Anglo-American tradition. It seems to me that there is a rhetorical tendency to portray Objectivism as having some "outsider" status, alienated from the mainstream. Much in the way that Howard Roark and John Galt were consummate outsiders, the dialectical situation is most romantically drawn as "one versus all"; there is often a pleasant frisson in seeing one's ideas as being opposed to tradition regardless of how well they, in fact, fit in.

I could be very wrong, but I see some of this rhetorical slant in how Khawaja views his project. He writes that he is offering an "account of analytic versus Objectivist approaches to the foundations of ethics." The "versus" seems, to me, to be unnecessarily confrontational. He writes that his intent is to: "identify [Objectivism's] overarching justificatory structure in such a way as to show . . . how it is in competition with analytic philosophy on problems that analytic philosophers can recognize as their own." Objectivism, he thinks, answers these questions in an importantly original way. He claims that the Objectivist take on metaethics and epistemology is supposed not to be readily assimilated into the philosophic tradition, but is rather supposed to exist in a "blind spot," and that "space" needs to be cleared for it. It is perhaps natural for egoists to see themselves as standing apart from and in competition with everyone else, especially when "egoism" may be attended by connotations of "heroism." Temperamentally, the egoist naturally resists "fitting in," but it is simply wrong to think that egoists have only existed in a blind spot of moral philosophy: Thrasymachus, Callicles, Machiavelli, Hobbes's Foole, Hume's Sensible Knave, and Nietzsche have to be familiar to anyone considering themselves even moderately familiar with moral philosophy. It would be unfair to say that Rand says nothing new to moral philosophy, but equally unfair to say that she is something revolutionary.

As understandable as the competitiveness may be, it is nothing but unfortunate from a purely philosophical point of view, which must be divorced from all romance. The philosophical goal is learning the truth so that one may act well; we should follow the argument even into the mainstream. Ignoring this can lead one astray by keeping one from seeing helpful similarities with the work of others, where the juxtapositions can be instructive, and where "the wheel" need not be reinvented over and over. Competition can tend toward confrontation, and while we must argue about the truth, we must not compete over it or mistake "winning" the argument as the goal. This is not a pragmatic way to pursue the truth. The philosophical attitude, as perhaps embodied by Socrates, will reject competition along with romance. This is not to say that Socrates may not be a romantic, perhaps competitive, or even heroic figure, only that these do not influence his search for the truth; here he retains his modesty in the face of facts to be discovered and not invented. This is philosophy as an unselfish love of truth and wisdom, where selfishness tends to bias judgment and lead away from objectivity.

I do not mean my arguments here to be ad hominem, but I think there are at least three philosophical problems arising from the competitive rhetorical style. If we make corrections to resolve them, I think it will promote a much better appreciation of how Rand stands to the rest of analytic moral philosophy, where she fits in, and what makes her position distinctive. While it lacks the romance, I think we will end up seeing her clearly and as not being quite the iconoclast that she is often seen as being.

The first problem concerns the typical subject matter of metaethics, which is typically understood in terms of a search for the metaphysics, epistemology, and semantics that makes best sense of various normative theories about how to live. The standard metaethical options on the table nowadays in analytic philosophy are, in rough terms, realism, expressivism, and error theories.[1]

Realism is a metaphysical doctrine, typically taken to involve the willingness to make an ontological claim about the existence of moral properties in the world which are, in some important sense, "mind independent." There are nonnaturalist and naturalist versions of realism.[2] Nonnaturalists, such as Moore (1993), Scanlon (1998), or Shafer-Landau (2003), typically think that moral properties require the same ontology that we give to reasons and rationality, where this is seen as resisting a naturalist's view of the world for the same reasons that logic and mathematics do. Naturalists, on the other hand, folks like Railton (1986), Foot (2001), and myself (see Bloomfield 2001), think that morality is a natural phenomenon, somehow either reducing to or emerging out of our nature as members of *Homo sapiens*. In general, realists see moral discourse as being truth-apt, where truth is understood as being more than deflationary, perhaps requiring some form of correspondence, where there are truth-makers in the world for our moral claims.

Expressivists or quasi-realists, such as Gibbard (1994) and Blackburn (1998), are the end result of a tradition that places the origins of morality in our sensibilities, emotions, or affective capacities. Theorists of this sort deny the ontological claim that the realists are willing to make, and think that moral claims are not assertions about the world but are expressions

---

1. Of course, I'm leaving out much. In particular, there are constructivist theories, which can be either like Kant (*Groundwork* [1998]) or Rawls (1999b) on one hand or explicitly relativist on the other. There are also hybrid theories, like the "cognitivist expressivism" of Terry Horgan and Mark Timmons (2006), or the marriage of a realist's ontology with an expressivist's view of moral language, like that proffered by David Copp (2001). I leave aside these for the sake of simplicity.

2. This dichotomy leaves out, I think, theories like that of David Wiggins (1987) and John McDowell (1988), who think that moral properties are secondary qualities like color, or are, in other terms, "response dependent." Whether or not these are really realist theories or some form of subjectivism that is masquerading as realism is part of the debate.

of attitude. Most people who currently write in this tradition do not try to reduce morality to affect, but see some role for cognition in morality, at least insofar as moral inferences must be accounted for.

Finally, error theorists, such as Mackie (1977), Garner (1990), and Joyce (2001) agree with realists and disagree with expressivists about the nature of moral language, for they see moral claims as being assertions that are capable of being true or false. On the other hand, they disagree with the realists and agree with the expressivists that truth-makers for moral claims do not exist. Error theorists think that moral claims purport to be assertions of items or entities in the world, but they think that no such items or entities exist. So, for error theorists, all moral claims are false.

Given this simplified picture of the metaethical lay of the land, it is not hard at all to see where Rand stands. It would be seemingly impossible to read her as either an expressivist or an error theorist, since she is easily identified as a realist. Moreover, it seems clear that she is a naturalistic realist and not a nonnaturalist, since she sees morality as being fundamentally due to the phenomenon of life. It is harder to say whether she would be a reductive naturalist, like most of the Cornell realists, or a nonreductive naturalist, more like Philippa Foot or myself.[3]

For a fairly traditional analytic metaethicist, which I am, what was most evident to me with regard to Khawaja's chapter was that these basic distinctions were not even mentioned; the metaphysics of morality and the semantic status of moral discourse were ignored. Instead, Khawaja discussed Rand's general epistemology, to which morality is supposed to be no exception. Of course, moral epistemology is of vital importance for a completed metaethic, but much of Khawaja's discussion of Rand's epistemology had no particularly metaethical implications. Rand is, apparently, some kind of foundationalist, which seems to be a perfectly respectable and mainstream view in epistemology, however she personalizes it. I think it is important that the marriage of a naturalist realism about moral properties with a foundationalist's general epistemology is a contingent one. The ontology does not, all by itself, seem to me to demand one epis-

---

3. In helpful communication, Allan Gotthelf has suggested that Rand's distinction between "objective" and "intrinsic" approaches to the good carves out a distinctive territory for her view (cf. *CUI* 13–16, and Darryl Wright's discussion in the present volume). This may be the case; I am not in a position to say. But there are rarely going to be two realists (or philosophers in general) who agree with each other on all the particulars, and I do not think it is unfair to paint Rand as warming herself around the same campfire as other naturalist realists.

temology over another; there is no necessary entailment that yields foundationalism out of a commitment to naturalistic realism.

It may perhaps be true that Rand's epistemology, in all its detail, does require one to be a naturalist realist with regard to moral ontology, but this would be to make epistemology Rand's "first philosophy," whereas it strikes me—non-expert that I am—that her claims about life are most closely allied with her egoism, and it is this latter that is most fundamental to her philosophy. If Rand took metaphysics as her first philosophy, as seems likely, then her epistemology must be seen in this light—as the result of theoretical decisions Rand made about how to best make sense of how we learn about the ontological facts of life and the moral facts about how to live it. Presumably, one could consistently adopt her views on life and how to live it and wed them to a coherentist's epistemology, involving a reflective equilibrium between theory and pretheoretical practice, or to a virtue epistemology, which says that moral claims, when justified, are justified by the fact that they were produced in accord with the intellectual virtues of honesty, perseverance, open-mindedness, etc. Unless I am missing something crucial, it seems to me as if Rand's epistemology, even her moral epistemology, is not theoretically necessitated by either her metaphysical or her moral views.[4]

Another way in which Rand fits more smoothly into analytic philosophy than she is portrayed concerns what might be called her conceptual analysis of morality. In particular, she adopts what W. D. Falk (1963) and William Frankena (1966) call a "formalist" conception of morality, in contrast to a substantivalist view of it.[5] A formal conception of morality is one which, at minimum, is prescriptive, that is, it tells one what one ought to do, and it overrides other operative normative frameworks. On this view, one's rule of life is one's moral code. Any action guide bearing these formal marks may count as a person's morality. The substantivalist's view, on the other hand, builds into the very concept of morality some substantive, normative, moral constraint, such as that the interests of others must be considered in moral decision making. If the formalist starts with the question "How should I live?" the substantivalist starts with (something like) the question "Why should I be moral?" where "being moral" entails taking other's interests into account (see also Baier 1970).

---

4. For further exploration one might consult *ITOE*. My thanks to Allan Gotthelf for discussion of these matters, on which we do not entirely agree.

5. For more discussion on the distinction between formal and substantive conceptions of morality, see Bloomfield 2008, introduction.

Rand writes, "a code of values accepted by choice is a code of morality" (*VOS* 16). On such a view, she would have to acknowledge that egoism, utilitarianism, deontology, and the ethics of care are all codes of morality, possible rules of life to live by, though of course she would not say that these are all equally good moralities or equally worthy of being a person's "rule of life." Egoism, as noted above, including Rand's version of it, is a going view among the traditional players in moral philosophy, even if it has not been a historically popular point of view. The distinction between formal and substantive conceptions of morality also explains why some people, namely those who start from a substantivalist's point of view, do not see egoism as a moral theory at all, since it does not commit itself to the relevance of other-regarding considerations in all moral deliberation. But egoists, Rand included, are not alone in being rejected by substantivalists as having "a moral philosophy," for on the substantivalist view, Rand is in the good company of all the Greek moral philosophers.

This can be easily seen by reading the opening dialogue between *In* and *Out* in Falk's "Morality, Self, and Others" (1963). Here is an extended quotation from Falk that should more than suffice:

> *In* [the formalist]: Not everyone will agree that as a moral being one has only commitments toward others or that only such commitments are properly "moral." The Greeks, for example, took a wider view. For Plato the equivalent of a moral being was the just or right-living person, and of a moral commitment the right and just course—the one which the right-living person would be led to take. And this right-living person was one who would keep himself in good shape as a sane and self-possessed being, and who would do whatever good and sufficient reasons directed him to do. This is why for Plato and the Greeks temperance and prudence were no less among the just man's commitments than paying his debts and not willfully harming others, and why the one was not treated as any less a moral commitment than the other. The Greeks placed the essence of man as a moral being in his capacity to direct himself on rational grounds; and his commitments as a moral being were therefore all those which he seriously incurred as a properly self-directing being.
>
> *Out* [the substantivalist]: Citing the Greeks only shows how distant their concept of morality is from ours. We will not call every rational commitment "moral" or equate the moral with the rational.

(In the foreword to Falk's collected papers [1986], Kurt Baier claims to have defended the *Out* position against Falk's *In*.) In any case, I think,

Falk has *In* articulating a view which, though perhaps distinct from Rand's in the normative particulars, clearly shares with her the idea that a morality is "what one lives by." And it is edifying to note, I think, that the paper this quote comes from was originally published in 1963, one year before *The Virtue of Selfishness* came out. Along similar lines, G. E. M. Anscombe's famous paper "Modern Moral Philosophy" came out in 1958, wherein she first heralded a dissatisfaction with the idea of "moral obligation" that had been handed down from the Scholastics to the twentieth century (see also Irwin 2008). So, while Rand did not, perhaps, fall within the mainstream of moral philosophy when she was writing in the 1960s, she was not arguing for a concept of *morality* that was unheard of at the time, whether she realized this or not. And indeed, she was using the same conception of morality that was at play in all Greek moral philosophy.

The final way in which I think it is wrong to see Rand as iconoclastic is more properly in the relation of her work to Greek eudaimonism. Of course we cannot hold Rand responsible for not appreciating recent work on virtue ethics that has shed light on Greek philosophy, but we can criticize her for writing of Aristotle: "he based his ethical system on observations of what the noble and wise men of his time chose to do, leaving unanswered the questions of: why they chose to do it and why he evaluated them as noble and wise" (*VOS* 14). It is hard to see this as close to a charitable reading of Aristotle, who first gave sense to how our reasons for acting can be unified by practical rationality and a concept of eudaimonia. And it is simply false to suggest that Aristotle did not even try to answer foundational questions regarding moral philosophy; indeed, Aristotle, more than anyone else, Socrates and Plato included, discerned the structure of eudaimonism and the theoretical underpinnings of what we now think of as "the good life."

I am aware that there is secondary literature on Rand and how her philosophy relates to Aristotelian teleology and eudaimonism, though I cannot claim to have gone through it. I know that some of our best work on teleology comes from philosophers who are intimately familiar with Rand's work. Are we supposed to imagine that Rand did not see her own work as having the same rough structure as the Greeks?

In fact, I think Rand's work can be seen as a paradigm of eudaimonism. Eudaimonism begins with the idea of a person having a sense of "one's life as a whole" and what Julia Annas calls a "formal" or "thin" conception of happiness (Annas 1993, Annas 2008). (This is a slightly different "formal/ substantive" distinction than Falk's and Frankena's.) This thin conception of happiness means that almost all the Greek moral philosophers accepted the idea that eudaimonia was the final end of human life, where "eudaimonia" is translated as "happiness" or "well-being" or "flourishing." Another way of phrasing this is to say that almost everyone agreed up front that the goal was to live the proverbial "good life" and all the debate was over what the good life is.[6] Epicurus said eudaimonia consisted of *ataraxia*, or tranquility, the absence of pain. The Stoics said that virtue was sufficient for the good life. Aristotle said that virtue was necessary but insufficient for the good life, and that certain external goods were also required. Insofar as all Greek moral philosophy began with the idea of an individual living a good life, it was all egoistic in a purely formal sense of the term.[7] One could then fill out a theory of the good life or eudaimonia in any number of ways, across a continuum of options, including perhaps at one end a life devoted to saintly beneficence and altruism, and at the other end a conventionally immoral life devoted to the self's best efforts at satisfying the actual needs, wants, and desires of the self regardless of their content. The saint, the villain, and everyone else all agree on wanting to live the good life, or eudaimonia; all the disagreement is about how this is to be done.

Rand naturally falls into such a continuum, though perhaps not quite as far toward the extreme as is often thought. There are various forms of egoism and Rand's is an unusually disciplined one; there are others, for example, who, unlike Rand, disregard considerations of virtue altogether. Thrasymachus can instructively be read as a eudaimonist, where his defense of *pleonexia* goes well beyond Rand's "virtue of selfishness."[8] Rand's version of egoism, I think, is more self-centered than one based on "enlightened self-interest," on at least most common understandings of what that is. In any case, Rand makes it clear that not all the desires a person might have are equally worthy of being pursued and satisfied and this makes her less extreme than she would otherwise be.[9] The impor-

6. The exceptions were the Skeptics, who would by practice accept no such principle, and the Cyrenaics, who were hedonists that rejected the idea of thinking of one's life as a whole.

7. For the charge that all eudaimonist theories are egoistic in a nonaltruistic, substantive (and pejorative) sense of that term, see Hurka 2001, chapter 8. For a response, see Annas 2008.

8. For Thrasymachus as a eudaimonist, see Annas 1981; see also Foot (2001) for a reading of Nietzsche as a eudaimonist with an idiosyncratic (and false) list of virtues.

9. See, for example, her discussion of looters and other "parasites" in *VOS* 23, also see "The 'Conflicts' of Men's Interests," *VOS*, chap. 4.

tant conclusion is that Rand's normative theory is not outside the scope of analytic metaethics in the least; she fits in just fine. One interesting question, worthy I think of a short digression before I conclude, is the degree to which Rand is in sympathy with the Stoics, especially if we ignore the Stoics' theory of passion and the emotions; after all, it seems safe to say that, speaking colloquially, both Roark and Galt were "Stoic" characters of heroic proportion.[10]

The Stoics, like Rand, viewed the answer to the question of "How to live?" by looking to nature and how it works. Their guiding prescription for eudaimonia was "live in agreement with nature." They too took human nature, as opposed to convention or culture, to set the constraints by which a human should live. They argued that virtue was sufficient for happiness, indeed their substantial take on virtue was governed by what would be required to live in accord with nature. Rand looked to nature to substantiate her theory of value as well, and, of course, she had her own version of virtue theory. Ultimately, of course, there are differences between Rand and the Stoics. These are not limited to what counts as "the virtues," but are, I think, most deeply distinct in regard to what counts as virtuous motivation. The Stoics thought that the virtuous person would always be motivated by the fine or the noble, *to kalon* in the Greek. This means that thoughts of what is best for oneself, the traditional egoistic motivation, are left out of the account. "Selfishness," assuming a common-sense understanding of the word, would not even have been a contender for being a virtue among the Stoics. Acting for the sake of others, especially when considerations of justice arise, would be a commonplace occurrence for a Stoic sage; the sage will appreciate that there are things in life worth dying for, the value of which is wholly outside the self and non-egoistic. it is hard to see Rand's selfish egoist agreeing. [11]

10. My brief and certainly incomplete search in the secondary literature came up with little on the topic of Rand and the Stoics, a developed juxtaposition of views which I think would be most interesting.

11. While there are other strands of Rand's writings that may appear to contradict this, it is not hard for most people to imagine scenarios in which refusal to unselfishly sacrifice one's life is shamefully ignoble. Rand writes at one point explicitly, "It is only in emergency situations that one should volunteer to help strangers, if it is in one's power. For instance, a man who values human life and is caught in a shipwreck, should help to save his fellow passengers (though not at the expense of his own life)" ("The Ethics of Emergencies," *VOS* 48). I thank Michael P. Lynch for pointing out this quote to me, and Allan Gotthelf for discussion with me on these matters. There is an interesting exchange on these topics between Christine Swanton and Darryl Wright in the present volume.

Of course, there is much to say about Rand's normative theory, its substantival use of egoism (as opposed to the formal use of it mentioned above), and the role that selfishness plays as, what seems to me, an overarching virtue in her theory. But this is neither the time nor the place for such discussion. I hope it is not too disappointing that I have said very little about epistemology in general or moral epistemology in particular. To that degree, I have not commented on a large measure of Khawaja's paper, and to that degree perhaps apologies are in order. My most significant concerns regarding his paper, as I hope I've made clear, have been to clarify Rand's relations to mainstream analytic philosophy and to reject any sort of competition between them. And, as I also hope I've made clear, I do not see Rand as being the outsider embodied in the most popular interpretation of her work by both her champions and her critics.

EGOISM AND VIRTUE IN NIETZSCHE AND RAND

Nietzsche and Rand as Virtuous Egoists

CHRISTINE SWANTON

I n the public mind, to be an egoist is to be immoral; in the philosophical mind, to be an ethical egoist is to adopt a form of immoralism. Yet as far as this equation goes, there is a problem in the interpretation of both Nietzsche and Ayn Rand. Both are self-styled egoists, yet the writings of both are replete with virtue and vice concepts, which are used substantively in the development of their moral views. In recent work, Tara Smith (2006) has gone a long way to resolving this conundrum. For her, there is a moral view that is a nontraditional form of virtue ethics, namely, virtuous egoism. This, according to Smith, is the view of Ayn Rand. I shall suggest that under one interpretation of virtuous egoism, virtuous egoism is also the view of Nietzsche. To argue this, we need to understand the notion of virtuous egoism, which in turn requires clarity about the possible forms of ethical egoism itself as a putative moral view.

There are two important dimensions along which versions of ethical egoism can be understood. The first concerns the application of the view to individual actions or, alternatively, to the pattern of one's life as a whole. Along the second dimension, egoistic views vary according to whether the egoism applies to motives or intentions of one's actions solely or to concepts such as benefit or sacrifice, which are not reducible to motives or intentions. I shall distinguish three versions of ethical egoism which are by no means exhaustive:

(E1) An agent should always be *motivated* by her own self-interest when she acts.

(E2) An agent should never *sacrifice* her own interests for the interests of another when she acts.

(E3) An agent should not organize her life as a whole around sacrifice for the sake of others, nor should her life exhibit a pattern of self-sacrifice.

(E2) does not entail (E1) for the following reason. Consider a mother who looks after her children well. She is not motivated by self-interest in so doing. However, in incurring costs, she may or may not be sacrificing her own interests for those of another. A sacrifice is not here understood simply as a cost. In Ayn Rand's sense, assumed here, a sacrifice occurs when one surrenders something of greater objective value to oneself for something of lesser objective value to oneself (*VOS* 50, cited in Smith 2006, 39). Assume that in looking after her children the mother does not sacrifice something of greater objective value to herself for something of lesser value, even though such care incurs considerable costs. Because of bonds of love, her own interests are bound up with the interests of her children. She has conformed to (E2) even though not to (E1); (E2) does not entail (E1).

(E3) does not entail (E2) for the following reason. Consider a soldier who lays down his life for his country. He is called upon to make the ulti-mate sacrifice. Now let us assume that, as Aristotle appears to recognize, even dying gloriously on the battlefield in a just war is a sacrifice in the sense defined above. (E2) has been violated. Yet, let us imagine, our sol-dier who has laid down his life for his country has not organized his life around self-sacrifice, because until he died, let us say, he was not charac-teristically sacrificing something of greater value to him than something of lesser value. The privations of the military life were costs, but not sacri-fices in the sense defined. (E3), then, does not entail (E2).

Corresponding to the three notions of egoism defined above are three notions of altruism, namely:

(A1a) One is sometimes permitted to be motivated by the interests of others.

(A1a) is simply the negation of (E1). However, according to Tara Smith, Rand's target is not the negation of (E1), but rather a much stronger version of altruism, which might be expressed as:

(A1b) One must always be motivated by the interests of others when one acts.

According to Smith: "E. J. Bond characterizes altruism as the policy of 'always denying oneself for the sake of others.' Burton Potter presents altruism as 'the position that one should always act for the welfare of others.' . . . Lawrence Blum observes that in its most prevalent usage, altruism refers to placing the interests of others ahead of one's own. This is clearly how Rand understands altruism" (Smith 2006, 38–39).

Corresponding to the second notion of egoism, (E2), is:

(A2) One is morally permitted, and may even be required, to sometimes sacrifice oneself for the sake of the interests of others when one acts.

Finally, corresponding to (E3) we have:

(A3) One must organize one's life around service to others where one may be required to sacrifice one's interests; or at the least, one's life must exhibit a pattern of service to others where one may be required to sacrifice one's interests, on a more or less ongoing basis.

(A3) is not always distinguished from the stronger position (A1b). Indeed Peikoff's understanding of Rand's target (1991, 240), as described by Smith, seems ambiguous between these positions: "Peikoff stresses that altruism is not a synonym for kindness, generosity, or good will, but the 'doctrine that man should place others above self as the fundamental rule of life'" (Smith 2006, 39).

We turn now to the notion of virtuous egoism. The idea that there can be a virtuous egoism has most plausibility when applied to (E2) and (E3). We may understand the corresponding senses of virtuous egoism thus:

(VE2) Although it may be virtuous to incur costs for the sake of another, it is never virtuous to sacrifice one's interests for the sake of another when one acts.

(VE3) A life exhibiting a pattern of self-sacrifice, or a life organized around such a pattern, is not a virtuous life.

(VE2) and (VE3) differ from their counterpart versions of ethical egoism only in that deontological concepts are replaced by virtue concepts. The task of a theory of virtuous egoism, as understood through the writings of Nietzsche and Rand, is to understand egoism through the virtue concepts, thereby providing a richer, deeper, explanation of the appeal of the favored form of egoism. In this way, the unattractiveness of the baldly deontological positions (E1) through (E3) may be mitigated.

The remainder of the paper proceeds as follows: I describe both Rand's and Nietzsche's versions of virtuous egoism, then point out an apparent difficulty with Rand's version, which may be resolved by appealing to the depth-motivational aspects of Nietzsche's notion of virtue and virtuous and nonvirtuous incurring of personal costs.

Rand's Virtuous Egoism

According to Tara Smith, for Rand, egoism is: "the paramount commitment to one's own wellbeing" (Smith 2006, 24). More precisely, it is the view that each person's primary moral obligation is to achieve his own well-being and he should not sacrifice his well-being for the well-being of others (23).

This characterization is ambiguous between (E2) and (E3): it is unclear whether the "primary moral obligation" relates to the pattern of one's life as a whole or to individual actions. I shall assume the stronger reading is Rand's intention. On either reading, understanding Rand's view requires a grasp of her notions of sacrifice and self interest. Recall that a "sacrifice" occurs in Rand's sense when one surrenders something of greater (objective) value to oneself for something of lesser (objective) value to oneself. Your interests are constituted by what is of objective value to you. But why should such a view be called *virtuous* egoism? The understanding of ethical egoism in terms of (VE2) is effected by three important moves. These are:

(i)   What is of "value" is what is of value *for an individual*. There are no "values" independent of what is valuable for an individual, though there is a *standard* of value independent of any individual's desires or preferences: "The Objectivist ethics holds man's life as the standard of value—and his own life as the ethical purpose of every individual man" (*VOS* 27).

(ii) What constitutes one's own interests or well-being is determined by *objective* values (for one): one's own beliefs and desires do not necessarily determine what is in one's interests.

(iii) Since what counts as an objective value is determined in part by virtue concepts (e.g., honesty, integrity, virtuous productivity, and justice), what counts as something being in one's interests is determined at least in part by *virtue*, and what counts as a genuine sacrifice to one's interests or well-being is determined, at least in part, by virtue.

Whether the idea of virtue determining, at least in part, one's interests is instrumental or constitutive is a difficult issue beyond the scope of this paper. It is clear, however, that for Rand's Roark, the architect of *The Fountainhead*, poverty as such is not necessarily damaging to his interests while in the service of virtuous pursuit of his artistic ideals, but having his phone cut off as a result of his poverty is damaging if it means he cannot pursue his creative ends as a consequence. Again, it is not against one's interests to refrain from being dishonest, thereby failing to secure a job for which one is not qualified or is otherwise undeserved given other candidates, but which one might have gained through dishonesty.

(VE2) as it pertains to Rand, then, should be understood as:

(RVE2) One should not benefit another if that constitutes a personal sacrifice, where a personal sacrifice is to be understood as a sacrifice of something of greater (objective) value to one for something of lesser (objective) value to one, and what has objective value to one is determined, at least in part, by virtue.

The question now arises: is (RVE2) (Rand's virtuous egoism) compatible with an acceptable altruism? It would appear so, since, as Smith points out, Rand is happy with virtuous actions benefiting others, and would therefore subscribe to the following version of what we might call virtuous altruism:

(VA) One should benefit another if and only if that is virtuous (that is, instantiates a virtue such as generosity, kindness, friendship, parental virtue, and so forth), or is at least compatible with virtue.

Note, however, that for the other-regarding virtues to be virtues for Rand, the incurring of personal costs in one's generosity for example, must be compatible with (VE2) or (VE3): the costs cannot be a sacrifice for her, or at the least, cannot exhibit a pattern of sacrifice.

Here is an example from Smith about how (VA) could be instantiated on Rand's view: "We can easily imagine the teacher being generous with his time, staying beyond the scheduled sessions to work with the student, without its being a sacrifice. If he greatly values the student's development and giving his best possible performance and if he can spare the resources on a given afternoon to go overtime, it can be in his interest to give the student more attention than the student could reasonably demand or expect" (Smith 2006, 258). In other words, generosity is not a sacrifice, other things being equal, if you have a stake in the interests of the beneficiary. You have a stake in others' or another's interests if, for example, you love another or value his success or well-being, or if helping others is part of your own creative and productive goals. So, it appears that for Rand, virtuous altruism (VA) is compatible with (RVE2).

But is Rand's conception of (VA) acceptable? Smith emphasizes that at the core of Rand's conception of (VA) is the rejection of the thesis that need alone may create moral demands on a person who is able to satisfy them. The question in my mind is this: Is there any room in Rand to criticize a person for having, relative to her circumstances, an excessively narrow conception of persons in whose interests she has some kind of stake? Is there something missing from Rand's version of altruism? There are two grounds for worry:

> (a) Are generosity and helpfulness virtues only if the generosity and the helpfulness are non-sacrificing (in Rand's sense) to a *virtuous* agent?

> (b) Even if the first question is answered in the affirmative, how should we understand the notion of sacrifice in nonvirtuous agents? How does (RVE2) apply here?

Consider a mother with attachment failures or difficulties. Working hard for her child's welfare is, from her subjective point of view, a sacrifice. Can such an agent be virtuous for Rand? Assuming that such an agent is not virtuous, what counts as being in the objective interests of such an imperfect agent? Could it in fact be in her objective interests to curtail certain of her very demanding productive activities for the sake of the child? Finally, given that such curtailment would arguably be a sacrifice for such an agent, would a virtue of parental generosity demand such a sacrifice, even though generosity should not demand sacrifice in the *virtuous*? Generosity should not demand sacrifice by the virtuous on this view because the virtuous, ex hypothesi, do not have an excessively narrow conception of those in whose interests they have a stake.

I shall leave these questions dangling and move to Nietzsche, before turning once more to them.

Nietzsche's Virtuous Egoism

Nietzsche is best read as a virtuous egoist in the sense of (VE3). The core of his view may be expressed as a version of (E3):

(NE3): The fundamental shape of an individual's life ought to be one where her *own* life is "enhanced" by her.

(NE3) is different from the following claim:

(NA): Everyone should affirm *life* overall.

(NE3) does not imply that one should affirm lives, whether one's own or others', no matter how mediocre. The idea of "self-overcoming," so prominent in Nietzsche, suggests that affirmation should be understood in terms of enhancement of one's own life, not uncritical acceptance of all lives. (NE3) also concerns a first-person perspective—that of the attitude one should have to one's own life. For this reason, (NE3) should also be distinguished from:

(NA') Everyone should affirm the best or superior lives.

Affirmation of others' lives, understood as admiration, is fine for Nietzsche; indeed one needs exemplars in "self-overcoming." However, (NE3) advocates dealing with one's *own* life rather than merely appreciating the admirable lives of others.

How can Nietzsche's egoism be read as a version of *virtuous* egoism? For, it may be claimed, the way to affirm one's own life for Nietzsche is to express, indeed maximize, one's "will to power," and this is hardly the route to a virtuous life. The ultimate concern of a life for Nietzsche, it may be thought, should not be a virtue, but power. I shall accept that for Nietzsche enhancing one's life is to be understood in terms of will to power, but also claim that the life-affirming life is one in which one's will to power is *undistorted*. That notion, in turn, is to be understood through the concepts of virtue and vice. In short, I shall argue for the following reading of (NE3) for Nietzsche:

(NVE3) The fundamental shape of an individual's life ought to be one in which that life is affirmed or enhanced, and genuine enhancement occurs only if she expresses her "will to power" in a way that manifests or expresses virtue, or at least does not manifest or express vice.

(NVE3) is egoist in that the requirement has to do with the enhancement of an individual's *own* life. The egoism is of the third kind since it has to do with the shape of the individual's life as a whole, as in (E3). Finally, the egoism is virtuous in that the driving force for Nietzsche, "will to power," must be undistorted; that is, it must be virtuous or at least not vicious, as in (VE3).

The task now is to show that Nietzsche can be understood as a *virtuous* egoist, and more specifically as subscribing to (NVE3). We need to show, first, how Nietzsche can plausibly be seen as some form of virtue ethicist given that *value* seems to be a core notion for him; and, second, that there is a connection between that virtue-centered morality and "will to power." Why should Nietzsche be understood as supporting (NVE3), given that he appears to valorize expressing our "will to power" by maximizing our own power?

Like Rand, Nietzsche appears to be a value-centered theorist. This is not surprising, since Nietzsche speaks of the revaluation of values and of the need to determine the rank order of values (1974, 345). If we are to ascribe to Nietzsche a virtue-centered morality, then we need to clarify, as with Rand, the relation between value and virtue. One might challenge the value-centered picture of Nietzsche on the grounds that for Nietzsche values are not entirely specifiable independently of virtue. It is not the case, for example, that power, pleasure, and truth are "values," let alone ones that need to be maximized. Pursuit of truth is valuable or good insofar as it is, for example, courageous, exhibiting hardness, and so forth (see May 1999, 188). By the same token, falsification may be valuable insofar as it is expressive of virtuous creative activity. Nor can we understand these aretaic notions themselves in terms of universal principles, for that is precluded by the complexity and holistic nature of the particular situations and motives in which these aretaic notions apply.

Given Nietzsche's doctrine of will to power, however, the most challenging task in ascribing to Nietzsche a virtue-centered morality is showing how his norms of power, indeed will to power, are infused with virtue. Huge portions of Nietzsche's philosophy, notably his mature ethical works *Beyond Good and Evil* and *The Genealogy of Morals*, give accounts of the varieties of distorted will to power that underlie various vices. This idea plays a central role in his view that psychology should be reinstated as the "queen of the sciences," for psychology can uncover the "depths" of our being, unlike traditional moral philosophy, which focuses on consequences and/or "surface" intentions, and which he regards as superficial.

Accordingly, psychology has to be regarded as "the road to fundamental problems" (1973, sec. 23, 54). In Nietzsche's words: "All psychology has hitherto remained anchored to moral prejudices and timidities: it has not ventured into the depths. To conceive it as morphology and the *development-theory of the will to power*, as I conceive it—has never yet so much as entered the mind of anyone else" (1973, sec. 23, 53).

For Nietzsche, the mature, strong individual is one who does not manifest the various distortions of will to power involved in a range of psychological defects underlying much vice. These defects, such as the resentment of the weak and powerless, resignatory forms of escape from the pleasures of the flesh, desire for intellectual purity, and subtle revenge against the suffering (who make one vividly aware of one's own vulnerabilities), underlie vices such as punitive rigorism and what Nietzsche calls "scientific fairness" (both distortions of justice as a virtue compatible with grace) (Nietzsche 1996, essay 2); intellectual vices of what I have elsewhere called hyperobjectivity (Swanton 2003, chap. 8); and pity, as opposed to what Nietzsche calls the virtue of sympathy (1973, sec. 284, 214).

To understand how Nietzsche's egoism can be understood as a species of virtuous egoism, then, we need to (very briefly) explain the nature and moral theoretic importance of will to power. Nietzsche's rejection of hedonism (the idea that only pleasure is intrinsically good) in his mature works is well known; what is not so well appreciated is that in his mature works goodness (or value) is not to be understood through the idea of will to power (as such) either. It is rather to be understood through the idea of will to power exercised well or excellently. The idea of "good" or "excellence" here is best or most substantively understood through Nietzsche's accounts of the variety of ways in which will to power can be defective or distorted. A virtue ethics based on the idea of will to power will thus require that an agent not express or enhance her will to power or power as such, but what I call "undistorted" will to power. That notion, in turn, is normative in a sense central to ethics, for undistorted will to power expresses or is at the core of virtue, or at least does not express vice.

Will to power as a general notion in Nietzsche should be understood as a genus, as opposed to various of its species. As a genus, it is a highly general idea, applicable to all life forms, as he writes: "A living thing desires above all to vent its strength—life as such is will to power" (1973, sec. 13, 44), and also "it will want to grow, expand, draw to itself, gain ascendancy—not out of any morality or immorality but because it *lives*, and because life *is* will to power" (1973, sec. 259, 194). As applied to humans, the need to "vent one's strength," or expand, is connected essentially with their nature as active, growing, developing beings; hence it is important to understand will to power in the context of what Nietzsche calls "the developmental psychology of will to power."

Will to power does not consist of something called the will, let alone a will to a single thing, power. "The will" is not to be understood as a single metaphysical entity belonging to an "indifferent substratum" that, via the operation of the will, produces bits of behavior as effects. Such a "will" is, for Nietzsche, a metaphysical fiction. A will *to power*, therefore, cannot be understood as a property of such a will. There is no will that is driving to a single thing, power, but rather agents who are weak or strong who vent their strength (or relative lack of strength) accordingly. As Nietzsche puts it, "unfree will" is mythology; in real life it is only a matter of "*strong and weak* wills" (1973, sec. 21, 51). If free will is mythology, so is unfree will, for there is no such thing as a will in that sense.

Will to power should not be understood as the product of a metaphysical entity called the will; it should also not be understood as a single motive. Nietzsche speaks frequently of the will to knowledge, the will to memory, the will to truth, the will to justice, and so on. The issue is whether such strivings (for truth and so on) are weak and distorted or are expressive of strong and full personalities.

To conclude this brief account: distorted will to power, which takes a variety of forms (illustrated in, notably, *The Genealogy of Morals*), underlies vice. Such vice is paradigmatically a depth-motivational phenomenon, which is expressed in actions. Virtue is marked by an absence of such distortion, or by motives or expressive features more positively valuable, noble, or admirable. Pity as a vice can thereby be distinguished from virtuous altruism, which Nietzsche frequently calls "overflowing"; resignation or "willessness" distinguished from sublimation; justice from resentment-based "scientific fairness"; and so on.

We are now in a position to see how Nietzsche's egoism can be described as a species of virtuous egoism. The expressive character of our actions as strong or weak makes sense of a claim that some actions that Nietzsche calls egoistic can be valuable. The notion of strong and weak wills gives us a clue about the source of this value, namely the character, or deeper drives or motives, of which actions are expressions. If a loving action, say, is expressive of being "overfull" and a neediness to bestow, then it is "egoistic" in a valuable sense. Such a person gives from a position of psychological strength as opposed to a self-sacrificial need to escape into otherness. The latter giver, who is empty and needs to be filled, is not affirming or enhancing her own life, but is rather externalizing self-contempt by loving for and through others.

Nietzsche, Rand, and Virtuous Altruism

Nietzsche's insights can be employed in a way that I think is sympathetic to Rand, to resolve the problem of "selfishness" in the sense of people having too narrow a conception of those in whose interests they have a stake. On some interpretations of Nietzsche, Nietzsche advocates that people have identifications well beyond themselves and narrow concerns: indeed, he has even been interpreted as a communitarian thinker.

In *Nietzsche's Philosophy of Religion*, Julian Young claims that Nietzsche's writings embody "*communitarian* thinking in the sense that the highest object of its concern is the flourishing of the community as a whole" (Young 2006, 1). Call this view:

(C) The highest value is the flourishing of the community as a whole.

Much of Nietzsche's writings support this reading, with his frequent claims that mediocrity (of culture or society) is the greatest ugliness. Superficially, (C) may be thought incompatible with egoism, virtuous or otherwise, but I shall deny that (NVE3) is incompatible with (C) on two broad grounds.

> (1) Even if the highest value is the flourishing of society, not every individual should affirm *his own* life by direct involvement in the redemption of society, and the removal of the "ugliness" in society's culture.

> (2) Having a social identity is interpreted as having a stake in the interests of one's society, and in its cultural health as a society with a heritage, but which needs to progress.

Attention to (1) and (2) allows us to integrate the egoist and communitarian aspects of Nietzsche's thought. Consider the following passages from *Zarathustra*:

> I love him whose soul squanders itself, who wants no thanks and returns none: for he always gives away and does not want to preserve himself.
>
> I love him whose soul is overfull, so that he forgets himself, and all things are in him: thus all things spell his going under. (1976a, pt. 1, sec. 4, 127–28)

These passages show that, for Nietzsche, higher types of human being have a stake in the flourishing of society as a whole, and in their capacities as leaders are directly concerned with that flourishing. Nietzsche does allow for the talented few to be directly involved in the flourishing of society as a whole: "the third *Meditation* is . . . addressed . . . to a "'small . . . band'" who, "through continual purification and mutual support . . . help prepare within themselves and around them" for the redemption of culture (1997, III, 6, qtd. in Young 2006, 46).

For Nietzsche, action in the service of this goal by such people, even where involving considerable personal cost, is not to be seen as life denying: it is not a case where the self "wilts away," and one "no longer knows how to *find* [one's] advantage" (1976b, sec. 35, 535–36). However, it is less clear that for Nietzsche *all* forms of sacrificing what is of greater personal value to what is of lesser value (to others, cultural progress, and so on) exhibit weak self-sacrifice. Incurring costs, even in the service of ends with which one identifies, could count as weak grandiosity violating the injunction "Do not be virtuous beyond your strength!" (1976b, pt. 4, sec. 13, 403), or a weak submerging of oneself into the collectivity in the service of ends one has not rationally and independently chosen.

It may be thought that the life affirmation of the average person is straightforwardly egoistic, but even for the average person, life affirmation does not occur in isolation from the culture, heritage, and roles that constitute the social identity of the individual. The communitarian elements in Nietzsche thus leave room for a critique of those who, while affirming their own lives, do not realize that, in Nietzsche's own words, they are "collective individuals" (1984, sect. 94, 65). Such individuals have an excessively narrow conception of those in whose interests they have a stake.

I have ascribed to Nietzsche a conception of social identity that grounds a requirement of virtue to have a stake in the interests of one's society and culture. Recognition of that identity is compatible with a range of activities commensurate with one's type (as, e.g., higher), role (as, e.g., cultural leader), and individual forms of creativity and productivity. If this is so, his egoism does not succumb to the criticism I previously potentially directed at Rand. But what of Rand herself? Can Rand reply to an objection that a person cannot be criticized for having too narrow a conception of those in whose interests she has a stake?

To deal with such an objection, Rand needs to argue that it may be in a person's objective interests to widen her conception of those in whose interests she has a stake. Note that such an argument will be highly contextual, taking account of a person's situation, talents, personality, the possibility of improvement, and so forth. Rand's notion of the second-hander suggests that, for her, some identifications with others or with society at large are expressive of weakness and of a deep-seated self contempt. Similarly, could she not argue that some *failures* to identify with others are also flawed—expressive perhaps of a deplorable failure of empathy, which is itself expressive of weaknesses of various kinds including a sense of personal worthlessness? Could she not criticize a selfish person who does not identify with broader concerns, people, and ideals on grounds similar to Nietzsche's? Such a move seems to me to be in the spirit of Rand's virtuous egoism. In-depth psychological analysis of characters is certainly not foreign to Rand, as her development of Dominique Francon's character shows. As Andrew Bernstein (2007) argues, Dominique's love for Roark is expressed in a distorted way precisely because it betrays a subconscious conflict between that love and her deep-seated pessimism about the success of people worthy of such a love.

It could be argued that any kind of identification with others or broader concerns is anathema to Rand. According to Onkar Ghate (2007, 245), Roark's "basic *motivation* in life is completely unconcerned with and unaffected by other people. His goal and his pursuit of it are purely independent and selfish." Rand's definition of independence as a virtue is "one's acceptance of the responsibility of forming one's own judgments and of living by the work of one's own mind" (*VOS* 28), a definition that is expanded upon in John Galt's speech in *Atlas Shrugged*. But her conception of independence does not entail being "unconcerned with" and being "unaffected by" other people. What is admirable about Roark is the fact that his independence is of a certain, virtuous sort, expressive of *proper* pride. It is not that he is unaffected by people simply, or that he does not care about them; rather he is not ruled by them, does not seek their approval, does not rely on their approbation for his self-esteem. Most importantly, his endeavors and his motivation are not dependent on *comparisons* with others. Contrast a form of nonvirtuous independence exhibited by Gail Wynand. He too is unconcerned with other people, in a sense, but his independence takes the form of loathing people, wanting to rule them, and of being callous toward them. In Nietzsche's terms, his will to power is distorted, motivated at a deep level by fear and pessimism rooted in his childhood experiences. The fear takes a much more independent form than that of Peter Keating, obviously: but it too is expressive of a form of what Alfred Adler would call an inferiority complex. In short, I see in Rand's novels a good deal of Nietzschean depth psychology, and it is in these terms that we should understand her concepts of virtuous egoism.

I conclude with the following remark concerning the questions posed at the end of my initial section on "Rand's Virtuous Egoism." Rand could argue that the "independence" of a person with distorted attachment, that is, the productive mother in my previous example, is not necessarily manifesting independence as a virtue. Is there a blueprint in any virtue ethics about how exactly various nonvirtuous agents should behave in a pursuit of virtue, or greater virtue? No, there is not, and there should not be.[1]

---

1. I would like to thank Darryl Wright for his excellent and interesting response. I wish to reply to one point. Citing Rand (*VOS* 28), Wright claims: "Neglecting the welfare of a child would be a pretty spectacular example of not assuming full responsibility for the effects of one's actions." In the passage cited, Rand argues for taking responsibility in the sense of never enacting causes without taking causal responsibility for the effects—no wishful thinking or mysticism is allowed. She does not here help herself illegitimately to a "moral point of view" such as Kant's motive of duty or Hume's "moral sense," which presupposes the existence of an "original passion" of benevolence (desire for the good of another) strengthened by a psychological capacity for extensive sympathy. It seems to me that a mother afflicted with the psychology of Kant's "unsympathetic moralist" of the *Groundwork*, could take responsibility in Rand's sense for her neglect, but unlike Kant's unsympathetic moralist, has no motive of Kantian duty to fall back on.

Virtue and Sacrifice:

Response to Swanton

DARRYL WRIGHT

In the preceding chapter in this volume, Professor Swanton has raised a fascinating question about Rand's ethics and looked at Nietzsche for thoughts toward an answer that she believes would also be congenial to Rand. The question is: Can you be faulted for insufficient engagement with the interests of others? And if you can, what then becomes of the principle in Rand's ethics that you should not make sacrifices for other people? For the insufficiently engaged, better engagement would seem to require sacrifice, whereas nonsacrifice would reinforce an already objectionable state of affairs. What guidance does Rand's ethics offer for such agents?

I think Swanton is correct in suggesting, "Rand needs to argue that it may be in a person's objective interests to widen her conception of those in whose interests she has a stake" and that Rand can indeed "argue that some *failures* to identify with others are . . . flawed—expressive perhaps of a deplorable failure of empathy, which is itself expressive of weaknesses of various kinds including a sense of personal worthlessness." Both of these general sorts of positions can be found in Rand's views about human relationships. As an example of the first, there is Rand's analysis of the personality type she calls the "tribal lone wolf" in her essay "Selfishness Without a Self." This sort of person is entirely alienated from other human beings, and Rand attributes his condition to a fundamental sort of selflessness—a lack of those personal values that constitute a "self" (*PWNI* 46–51). As an example of the second, there is the character of Ellsworth Toohey in *The Fountainhead,* whose hatred of all creative and independent people is borne of a deep-seated sense of worthlessness and inferiority.

The Sacrifices of Nonideal Agents

Swanton imagines a woman with attachment difficulties who values her career above the best interests of her child, and thus chooses to work more than her financial needs require. In effect, Swanton points out an inconsistency among three claims:

(i) It is wrong to make a sacrifice.

(ii) It is not wrong for the woman to take good care of her child.

(iii) It would be a sacrifice for the woman to take good care of her child.

These look like they cannot all be true, but it may seem that Rand is directly committed to (i) and—in the case Swanton stipulates—would be hard-pressed to reject either (ii) or (iii). So what to do?

Consider (i). After defining a sacrifice as "the surrender of a greater value for the sake of a lesser one or of a nonvalue," Rand says the following:

> The rational principle of conduct is the exact opposite: always act in accordance with the hierarchy of your values, and never sacrifice a greater value to a lesser one.
>
> This applies to all choices including one's actions toward other men. It requires that one possess a defined hierarchy of *rational* values (values chosen and validated by a rational standard). Without such a hierarchy, neither rational conduct nor considered value judgments nor moral choices are possible. (*VOS* 50)

For ease of reference, let us call the principle of conduct stated in the first sentence of this passage *R*. For Rand, adherence to *R* is an aspect of the virtue of rationality; it is one of the principles to which a person possessing this virtue is committed.[1] The principle's virtue-constituting status is

---

1. I take it that this commitment might only be implicit; that is, not one that the person himself could articulate in these terms but one that we could attribute in view of his characteristic ways of deliberating and making decisions. Further, I take it that a person whom we would properly consider to have the virtue of rationality, as Rand understands it, might

important for the following reason. In Rand's ethics, what is normative, in the first instance, is not the freestanding principle itself but the entire virtue that the principle helps constitute. Thus, it is also part of the virtue of rationality to choose and validate one's values by a rational standard and, as part of that process, to integrate one's values into a "defined hierarchy." (I say "as part of that process" because it seems to me that the validating and the hierarchical ordering of one's values cannot be wholly separate issues—to relate a value to a standard is per se to gain at least some sense of its importance in relation to that standard and in relation to one's other values.) And R comes into force as part of the virtue of rationality for a person who (possessing this virtue) has a "defined hierarchy of rational values" by reference to which to apply R. But R does not have any (virtue-) independent normative force; it is not a principle that obligates us (even qua having made the choice to live, which Rand makes part of the basis of morality) all by itself. This, I think, is part of why virtue concepts are important in Rand's ethics. They supply the framework needed for integrating and contextualizing different moral principles. The principles are important as well, since they permit us to identify and respond appropriately to the morally salient dimensions of any given choice we may face. But without the integrating context supplied by virtue concepts, that more fine-grained attempt to identify morally salient dimensions would have no means of avoiding misconceptualizations—that is, the grouping together of essentially different cases under a single principle.

This is what would be happening if, taking R to be a freestanding principle of conduct, we judged that the woman in our example, however she came by her values, would (for Rand) be making a wrongful sacrifice if she reduced her demanding work schedule in order to take care of her child. If her values are not rational, then that conclusion cannot be drawn, on Rand's view. Does it follow, then, that she would be making a rightful or morally permissible sacrifice? Let's postpone the moral evaluation of her action for a short while and focus first on its status relative to the concept of "sacrifice." It might seem that this concept is simply inapplicable here. According to the above passage, "neither rational conduct, nor considered value judgments nor moral choices are possible" without "a defined hierarchy of *rational* values." But if "considered value judg-

---

nevertheless fail due to a nonculpable lack of moral knowledge to do everything this virtue requires (such as to refrain from making sacrifices with respect to our rational and rationally prioritized values). But R is an aspect of rationality for Rand in the sense that it is part of a full specification of this virtue's nature and requirements.

ments" are impossible to the woman in our example, then a considered judgment that an action either would or wouldn't constitute a sacrifice is also impossible to her, since the latter type of judgment depends on prior value judgments. If that is the case, it would simply be indeterminate at this point what would or would not be a sacrifice for her. Let us call this the *strong conception of sacrifice* and explain it this way: a sacrifice can occur only when an agent acts against a *rational* hierarchy of personal values that he has formed.

On the strong conception of sacrifice, whether the woman in our example views taking care of her child as a sacrifice is neither here nor there. This is not to say the agent's point of view would have no relevance to the kinds of issues we are considering. Certainly, for Rand, an action's status as a sacrifice (or not) *does* depend on how it relates to the agent's own values, and these must be chosen by, not simply prescribed to, that agent. There is certainly no prospect of just reading off from morality plus circumstances what someone's hierarchy of values ought to look like, and then judging gains and sacrifices on that basis. Further, the person's own value-perspective—that is, his hierarchy of values and his judgments about how different courses of action would impact his values—is important for another reason. Rand's ethics does not demand that we (omnisciently) never act in a way that results in a net loss for us. In hindsight, we may see that we are worse off because of an action whose consequences were unforeseeable (e.g., a friend we had every reason to trust betrays us). That's not a sacrifice or any kind of moral issue, for Rand. So a sacrifice must be seen as such by the agent at the time of action—not necessarily in so many words, but in some way the agent must expect the action to result in a net loss to him given what he personally values. Or, alternatively, the loss must proceed from culpable ignorance on the agent's part (which would amount to the agent's not caring whether or not his values were protected and thus would also seem to belong in the category of making a sacrifice). But on the strong conception of sacrifice the fulfillment of one or the other of these two criteria—expecting a loss or culpable ignorance—is only a necessary and not a sufficient condition. The other necessary condition is that a person form his hierarchy of values rationally.

Does the strong conception of sacrifice have the unwelcome implication that only rational people are able to make sacrifices—at the same time that making sacrifices is supposed by Rand to be a hallmark of irrationality? In a sense it does: it implies that a sacrifice is a failure of rationality in an otherwise (substantially) rational person. But I do not see this as a problem for that conception or for the ascription of it to Rand; certainly she does not deny that people can be morally inconsistent. Nevertheless, there is reason to think that Rand does *not* hold the strong conception of sacrifice. For example, consider the following from Galt's speech in *Atlas Shrugged*: "If a mother buys food for her hungry child rather than a hat for herself, it is *not* a sacrifice: she values the child higher than the hat; but it is a sacrifice to the kind of mother whose higher value is the hat, who would prefer her child to starve and feeds him only from a sense of duty. If a man dies fighting for his own freedom, it is not a *sacrifice*: he is not willing to live as a slave; but it is a sacrifice to the kind of man who's willing" (*Atlas* 1029). The second case in each pair gives us a preference ordering that, to Rand, is not rational. But, according to Rand, both of these agents make sacrifices by acting against those preference orderings. This passage suggests what I will call the *weak conception of sacrifice*, on which making a sacrifice is forfeiting a higher value for the sake of a lower one, or a nonvalue, relative to one's own value hierarchy whether or not it is rational. Note that Rand does not say that agents with irrational value hierarchies should not make sacrifices. The provision from the other passage I quoted would still be in force: that is, *R* would still only be applicable in the context of rational values rationally prioritized. Rhetorically, the implication of the passage just quoted is that someone to whom the actions described would be sacrifices would be a contemptible person. For Rand, the fact that it would be a sacrifice for you to feed your child instead of buying a hat, or to fight for your freedom instead of living as a slave, shows that you are morally lacking. It precisely does not give you moral license to buy the hat or not fight.[2] According to the weak conception of sacrifice, the fact that you would be acting against ill-considered value judgments entails that your values have no moral weight; thus, morality would not sanction your conduct merely because it was in accord with your values.

Referring back to claims (i)–(iii), we have seen the sense in which Rand endorses (i), and we have seen, further, that (i) as endorsed by Rand has no immediate implications for the conduct of the woman in our example. Claim (i), as Rand espouses it, applies only in the context of a ra-

2. Indeed, Rand states, "Sacrifice could be proper only for those who have nothing to sacrifice—no values, no standards, no judgment—those whose desires are irrational whims, blindly conceived and lightly surrendered" (*Atlas* 1029). That is, such people would have no warrant for the uncompromising pursuit of what in their motivational systems takes the places of values.

tional value hierarchy, which the woman may not have. Or, to put this in terms of the virtues, (i) applies as a part of the specification of the virtues— primarily but not exclusively the virtue of rationality[3]—and we have yet to say anything about the woman's level of virtue. If she is not virtuous, (i) will not apply. What she needs to do in that case is to develop virtue, not just go on acting under the prompting of such values as she has.

Could the woman in our example rationally value working more than necessary at the expense of the best interests of her child? We are supposing that her attachment difficulties lead her to have the priorities she has. Could these priorities be rational for her? If she is in the grip of neurosis, then it is clear that Rand would consider her priorities to be irrational. But could the woman for any reason hold such priorities rationally in relatively normal kinds of circumstances (and let us perhaps unrealistically exclude the alterative of adoption, to focus the issue in the way that Swanton intends)? It seems to me that the short answer, from Rand's perspective, is that she could not. It would precisely be a failure of rationality for someone to have such priorities, if part of what the virtue of rationality demands is "that one must never enact a cause without assuming full responsibility for its effects" (*VOS* 28). Neglecting the welfare of a child one had chosen to have would be a pretty spectacular example of not assuming full responsibility for the effects of one's actions.[4] From a conventionally egoistic point of view, of course, one could ask why these particular effects should matter to the woman if she now prefers to go on working full-steam. But, for Rand, the virtue of rationality assigns the woman moral responsibility for the child she has brought into the world—it and its needs are her doing (and the father's, of course) and thus hers (as well as his) to bear the cost of—in money, time, effort, and emotional investment—even if she tragically lacks any maternal feelings and could not for whatever reason have arranged for the child to be adopted (or did not do so). Fundamentally, it is being rational in which the woman has an egoistic stake. I will comment a little further on this point in a moment, but I mention it here just by way of a reminder about the structure

3. *R* is also relevant to the virtues of honesty, integrity, justice, and pride. See *VOS*, chaps. 1 and 3, as well as *Atlas* 1019–21; also see Peikoff 1991, 284.

4. That said, there are some complicated issues to be worked out in this general area about what it means to assume (full) responsibility for the effects of one's actions, why one's actions having certain kinds of effects imposes certain kinds of responsibilities on one, and why this principle about responsibility is part of the overall virtue of rationality. My goal here is not to try to resolve any of these issues but only to provide a template of how Rand would go about answering the question Swanton's chapter raises.

of Rand's ethics. Her view is that there are egoistic reasons to be rational, and that the fundamental importance of this and the other moral virtues is such that they must set the terms of how one goes about gauging other benefits and losses.[5]

We have also dealt with claim (iii). If, as the material from Galt's speech suggested, Rand holds the weak conception of sacrifice, then she would agree with (iii). But certainly she would also consider it the woman's moral obligation to take good care of her child, and thus she would agree with (ii), as well. That means that, for Rand, the woman in the example would have a moral obligation to take action that would be a sacrifice for her. This is not to say that she has a moral obligation to make a sacrifice. Although she might just grudgingly force herself to do what was needed, she could also fulfill her obligations (and do so more completely) by rethinking and reshaping her hierarchy of values to make it more rational, and then carrying out her parental obligations in accordance with a revised value hierarchy in which these obligations entailed no sacrifices at all. More realistically, in the short term, perhaps, she might get herself to act nongrudgingly even before she understood very much about the conflict she felt between child-rearing and her career, or about the psychological problems that might lie beneath her inability to take a healthy interest in her child. She might say to herself, in effect, "OK, I've made a terrible mistake (or I have a terribly difficult psychological problem), I would actually rather be working than dealing with the demands of child-rearing, but this is what I must do, having brought into the world a child who is dependent on me." This would be a step toward understanding her moral obligation to take good care of her child in a non-self-sacrificing way. It would be a further step in this direction—a step toward understanding the egoistic benefits of rationality and morality—if she could begin to connect the taking of responsibility for the effects of her actions (and so for the needs of her child) with her own self-esteem (see *VOS* 29, 61–62; *PWNI* 100–101).

Things might not go nearly so well, of course. The woman might experience parenting as oppressive and fulfill its demands resentfully. Being moral, in this area of her life at least, might be a sacrifice to her. For Rand, this would not show that morality had lost its obligating force but that the woman was morally deficient. Rand's analysis of the moral deficiency of

5. Thus, discussing the virtue of honesty, Rand says that the honest person recognizes that "neither love nor fame nor cash is a value if obtained by fraud," i.e., by dishonest means (see *Atlas* 1019).

a person such as this would, of course, be an egoistic one. The deficiency, for Rand, consists in her inattentiveness to the real needs of her own well-being—here, primarily, inattentiveness to the psychological needs of her own life. To put it paradoxically, what's wrong with her is that not sacrificing herself is such a sacrifice.

Putting it this way brings out another sense of the concept of "sacrifice" that sometimes appears in Rand's writings, as, for instance, in this passage from her unfinished monograph *The Moral Basis of Individualism*: "The independence of man's mind means precisely the placing of his ego above any and all other men on earth. It means acting upon the authority of his ego above any other authority. It means keeping his ego untouched, uninfluenced, uncorrupted, *unsacrificed*" (*Journals* 260). In Rand's view, of course, someone lacking a rational hierarchy of values, and in other ways lacking with respect to the virtues, would fail to satisfy this characterization. He would fail to satisfy it even if he always acted according to his own value hierarchy.[6] By contrast, although the woman in Swanton's example would be making a sacrifice from the standpoint of her own values, if she fulfilled the demands of good parenting at the expense of her career, it could not be said that she was sacrificing her interests or her ego, if, as Rand would insist, it could not be to her interest to violate the requirements of morality. Provided that she did not just act grudgingly or out of duty (and perhaps even if she did[7]), she would be acting to strengthen and protect her own ego.

Altruism

Swanton attributes to Rand a thesis called "virtuous altruism" (hereafter VA). The thesis, as Swanton posits it, maintains: "One should benefit another if and only if that is virtuous (that is, instantiates a virtue such as generosity, kindness, friendship, parental virtue, and so forth), or is at least compatible with virtue." Although we should worry about the multiplication of virtue concepts in the interpretation of Rand, I will set that aside for now. There are two other problems with the attribution of VA to Rand.

6. A further issue here concerns the extent to which such a person could be said to have values, as opposed to mere whims; "values," as Rand uses the term, have a certain psychological stability that a very irrational person's motivating aims might not possess, and in that case it is doubtful that the concept of "sacrifice" as the surrender of a higher value for a lower one could be applicable at all.

7. Even if she did, she might still discover some of the psychological benefits of this kind of action, and be spurred to reevaluate her attitude toward it.

At best, VA is a thesis Rand holds incidentally, as a consequence of other views. It does not express the reason why she believes that helping someone may be morally required or morally right. On her view, the impetus for helping should derive from one's rational hierarchy of values. One helps because one's values require or at least permit it. The "because" here is both justificatory and motivational: the ideal moral agent, Rand holds, is guided by a rational hierarchy of values and it is the agent's values (qua rational) that justify the choices the agent makes. Included here is a generalized valuing of others on grounds of benevolence, which is sufficient to justify and motivate small acts of kindness toward strangers, such as holding a door or giving directions. In regard to those whose roles in the agent's life are larger and more important, the ideal agent's values will warrant and motivate a great deal more (see Wright 2011). The virtues have a role in shaping the agent's values; for instance, productiveness, independence, and pride will all in various ways influence what the agent will be willing to do for others. Thus, the agent will not, over the course of his entire life, treat relationships with others as more important than his own work, although another person may be his most important concern at a particular time; and the agent will not change his opinions to please his friends, or in any other way compromise his moral standards for them. The virtues may also directly motivate (and justify) the agent's action in the face of a morally difficult or ambiguous choice; further, the virtue of justice seems more likely than others to be an explicit focus of routine deliberation. But if we focus on the kinds of benefits that are not required by justice, the virtues alone do not directly determine whom one should benefit, on Rand's view; for that, a rationally formed hierarchy of personal values is necessary.

Another problem with the attribution of VA to Rand has to do with the concept of "altruism." I take it that Swanton intends "virtuous altruism" not merely as a label for the particular thesis that she specifies but also as a substantive characterization that makes contact with established understandings of the term "altruism." If it is only a label, then at any rate it is a confusing one to attach to a thesis being ascribed to Rand, since normally "altruism" refers not simply to beneficence but to unselfish beneficence, which is what Rand's ethics precludes. If it is a substantive characterization, however, then it is not entirely clear what "altruism" means such that there can be virtuous and nonvirtuous forms of it, on Rand's view. It can't mean "unselfish beneficence," since Rand considers that nonvirtuous in every case. If it just means "beneficence," then Swanton is adopting a looser usage that Rand objects to. Consider two actions: (a) an action that is taken for the benefit of someone else, but that has an underlying egoistic motivation, that is, a motivation having to do with the person's place in the agent's own hierarchy of values; and (b) an action that is taken for the benefit of someone else, and that has no underlying egoistic motivation but instead constitutes a sacrifice for the agent. Swanton reads Rand as holding that (a) is virtuous altruism and (b) is nonvirtuous altruism. But Rand considers it important to deny that (a) is any form of altruism at all (there's no dispute about [b]).

Rand sees a basic moral difference between (a) and (b), a difference that warrants a conceptual distinction—namely, that (b) is altruistic but (a) is not. By why does it warrant *this* conceptual distinction? Why wouldn't "virtuous versus nonvirtuous altruism" be enough of a distinction? To classify (a) and (b) as forms of altruism implies that they are united in a morally significant way. But that is exactly what Rand denies. To take one of the cases that she mentions in her essay "The Ethics of Emergencies," she denies that the man who spends a fortune to cure the illness of his beloved wife is, in any respect, acting on the same principle as he would be "[if] he let her die in order to spend his money on saving the lives of ten other women, none of whom meant anything to him" (*VOS* 51). Each of these actions, she holds, would be inconsistent in its governing principle with the other one; describing them both as altruism obscures what to her is a morally critical difference in the way in which the well-being of the "other" figures into the agent's reasons for acting.

My differences from Swanton's interpretation of Rand amount to saying that, in one way, the virtues have a more prominent role in Rand's thought than Swanton's account recognizes; but that, in another way, their role is less prominent. Further, I have stressed the problems with interpreting Rand as endorsing any form of altruism.[8]

8. On the issues of this discussion, see also the exchange between Swanton and Tara Smith in this volume.

AUTHOR
MEETS
CRITICS
Tara Smith's
Ayn Rand's
Normative
Ethics

This section, which will appear in Ayn Rand Society Philosophical Studies from time to time, presents the results of Ayn Rand Society sessions in which the author of a particular work responds to reflections on that work by other scholars. The Author Meets Critics section preserves the informality of such exchanges.

Rational Selves, Friends, and the Social Virtues

HELEN CULLYER

Tara Smith's *Ayn Rand's Normative Ethics* (2006) provides a subtle and challenging version of what it means to be an ethical egoist. The naturalistic basis of Rand's work, as presented by Smith, makes this egoistic theory one that should be taken seriously by moral philosophers, rather than simply dismissed. However, Rand's view of human nature as individualistic and contractual may be complicated and undermined by the recognition (made by Rand and Smith) of the importance in human life of common interests and shared activities that cannot be explained by the thesis that humans are by nature contractual beings. Smith's version of Rand's ethics actually suggests two quite different and incompatible models of egoism that I term the "rational maximizer" model and the "rational non-maximizer" model.[1]

Rand's virtues of independence, integrity, and pride, as explicated by Smith (2006, chaps. 5, 7, and 9), should be recognized as virtues by many who disagree with Rand's ethical egoism. Despite disputes about the logical basis of virtue and the goal of virtuous activity, many will agree that

1. See also my review of Smith's book (Cullyer 2006). Portions of this argument have appeared in that review. The review, however, has a different structure and broader focus than the current paper.

attaining and maintaining a virtuous disposition is difficult, and that we run the risk of failing through conceit or diffidence. Conceit may lead us to think that either a life lived according to beliefs that are unexamined (as Plato's Socrates would put it), or the life of a second-hander (as Rand would say) is a successful one. If we are diffident, we will drift through life out of "mental focus" (Smith 2006, 52), not caring whether we exhibit any consistent or coherent plan of action. Ancient philosophers such as Socrates, Aristotle, and the Stoics Epictetus and Musonius Rufus try to combat both tendencies by dialectical and rhetorical strategies that aim not to indoctrinate their audiences with ethical beliefs but rather to lead them to examine their own reasons for acting and to cultivate a self that *cares* about its reasons for acting. In fact, without the virtues of independence of judgment, loyalty to one's convictions (integrity), and respect for oneself and ambition to improve (pride), one could not accomplish much either for oneself or for others. Yet these self-regarding virtues are not merely instrumental in function and value. They also have a claim to some intrinsic value, if we think of them as dispositions whose exercise expresses the coherence and consistency of reasons and actions exhibited over the course of an individual's life.[2] Some aspects, then, of Rand's ethical ideal can be shared by Stoics, Aristotelians, Kantians and by all those who take virtue to be or to require a rational disposition. Self-esteem is valued even by Kant.[3]

2. One might object here that if an individual's life is marked by consistent and coherent reasons for acting, this shows that she is committed to certain principles and ideas, and thus she exhibits independence and integrity, but not necessarily pride. Why should pride be a virtue at all? As Smith explains, pride for Rand is "moral ambitiousness" directed towards perfecting oneself as a rational agent. It is a positive estimation of one's moral worth and builds self-esteem. Although pride and self-esteem are conceptually distinct, psychologically it is not a question of pride merely being a tool to build self-esteem; rather the two mutually reinforce each other (2006, 229n37). Without pride and self-esteem, as Smith argues, rational activity is crippled (229), but that is not because pride is a nonrational disposition or feeling that supports rational judgment. Rather pride is an aspect of rationality.

3. Thus Kant argues the following in his *Metaphysics of Morals*: "But from our capacity for internal lawgiving and from the (natural) human being's feeling himself compelled to revere the (moral) human being within his own person, at the same time there comes exaltation of the highest self-esteem, the feeling of his inner worth (*valor*), in terms of which he is above any price (*pretium*) and possesses an inalienable dignity (*dignitas interna*), which instills in him respect for himself (*reverentia*)" (Kant 1996, 187). Although Kant distinguishes the moral from animal self, and thinks that self-esteem must be combined with humility for the moral law (two ideas which Rand could certainly not endorse), it is important to remember that self-regard is not excluded from morality by Kant.

Moreover, the idea that enlightened self-interest can ground an ethical theory, although certainly rejected by many contemporary philosophers as Smith notes (1–2), is not foreign to the history of ethics and enjoys some prominence in ancient ethical theories. If we consider ethical egoism as the doctrine that one should always serve one's own interest by maximizing material goods for the self or by maximizing whatever one happens to desire, then egoism is a nonstarter, for it simply yields a picture of human life that few people in ancient or contemporary society could endorse as good. In such a life, all human associations exist for the sake of some utility or pleasure and predation of various kinds goes unchecked. But this is not Rand's picture, as Smith shows, for two reasons. What is of value to the self is not merely material (32); more importantly, the goal of life is for Rand to live in accordance with our human nature, i.e., to live as a rational animal. Self-care thus requires recognition of the reality of others and of their rights to life, liberty, and property. In fact, as Smith shows, Rand's view of ethical egoism is closer to an Aristotelian egocentric, agent-centered view of ethics than to many standard views of egoism countenanced by contemporary philosophers. The Randian view should be taken seriously by all those who think that it is more plausible to take as a starting point of ethical inquiry "what it is to be human," than it is to ground such inquiry in a collection of subjective assumptions, or in the idea that morality exists as absolute law (in the form of divine commands or a priori reasons).[4]

Smith suggests, in the first few chapters of her work, that Rand's ethical project is based on arguments about human happiness or flourishing (eudaimonia) and function that owe much to Aristotle's *Nicomachean Ethics*. Humans, just like animals or plants, have certain objective ends (food, water, safety) that promote our lives, but humans' ultimate goal is not only to survive, but to live well, which means excellent functioning, both physical and psychological (Smith 2006, 32) in accordance with rationality, our peculiarly human capacity. Since excellent functioning is the goal of human life, constituting our happiness/flourishing, and a person can only achieve this goal through her own rational efforts, reasons for acting must be egoistic (33). Moral principles are formed through a

---

4. The plausibility of a naturalistic view of ethics is one that I do not have space to argue for here. Obviously any appeal to naturalism comes with pitfalls and is open to abuse. Moreover, there is likely to be disagreement about what exactly constitutes human nature. For a good discussion of the pitfalls, problems, and benefits of such an approach, see Annas 2005.

series of inferences about the effects of different types of actions on human flourishing (35), and "the authority of moral principles stems entirely from their practical service to self-interest, as that is judged by rational, long-range standards" (36). It is also important to note that according to Rand, genuine self-interest cannot truly conflict with the interest of others (39).

Many philosophers who, like Rand and Smith, work in the Aristotelian tradition of eudaimonistic ethics will balk at the suggestion that if happiness is essentially rational activity, all one's first-order reasons for acting must be egoistic. The theoretical recognition that happiness is rational activity of the agent is logically compatible with the belief that it is rational to act, practically speaking, for the sake of others. In fact, despite the many similarities between Rand's eudaimonistic ethics and those of Aristotle and contemporary Aristotelians like Foot (2001) and Hursthouse (1999), Rand and Smith diverge from Aristotle and his other modern successors when it comes to the questions of what exactly constitutes human nature and what sorts of goods serve as the ends of rational activity. There is general agreement among Aristotelians that rational activity constitutes human goodness, but there is disagreement about the end or ends at which rational activity aims.[5]

For Rand, rationality aims at the creation and promotion of life-enhancing values for the individual (Smith 2006, 22). For most others in the Aristotelian tradition, the aims of rationality are more complicated. Scholars in this tradition would allow that it is rational for the individual qua animal to aim at her own maintenance, survival, and life-furthering activities, but other good reasons for acting exist. Aristotelians tend to think that character is formed in a social and political context; that human flourishing cannot be understood without considering individuals as parts of a community; and that as a result of ethical habituation and natural sociality we have reason to promote others' good. Thus, Foot (2001, 16) argues that humans are just particularly complex social animals, and she does not take the agent-centeredness of her ethical theory to entail that all of the virtuous agent's *reasons* for acting are egoistic. Aristotle himself asserts that the virtuous agent undertakes fine, virtuous actions for the sake of the fine (*to kalon*), i.e., for their own sake, because

---

5. This is what is particularly confusing about Aristotle's ethics. It is true to say that Aristotle and Aristotelians think that happiness is rational activity, but unless we identify some end or ends for reason to aim at as good, then we have not identified what makes rational activity *rational*.

they are fine. Fine actions are those that are contextually appropriate for and worthy of a socially and politically embedded individual.[6]

For Rand on the other hand, the moral self, while usually existing in a community, is self-created and independent of the community; humans are not by nature "social," though nor are they "lone wolves"; rather, they are "contractual" (Smith 2006, 130).[7] Smith endorses Rand's principle that it is never moral to put another's good above one's own and also asserts that "ethics is not essentially social" (284). There are three important claims here:

(1) Each individual exists by nature only for himself.[8]

(2) Human individuals do not by nature need to depend on others either materially or intellectually.[9]

6. Aristotle's claim in *Politics* I.2 that the individual is part of the state should not be taken to suggest that virtuous activity undertaken for the sake of *to kalon* is activity undertaken solely for the sake of the state. The range of virtuous activities considered in the *Ethics* simply does not support this, and ultimately Aristotle argues that the happiest life is the philosophical life rather than the life of politics. *Politics* I.2 suggests, when read with the *Ethics*, that human virtue cannot be understood without conceiving of individuals as embedded in a community, not that the community is the sole object to which virtue is dedicated.

7. Smith here quotes "A Nation's Unity—Part 2" *ARL* 3:2 (23 Oct. 1972). I take Rand's point here to be an explication of Akston's comment in *Atlas*: "man *is* a social being but not in the way that the looters preach" (747).

8. "Existing for oneself" seems to have two aspects in Rand. On one hand, in Rand's novels it often suggests an existential freedom of will; one is born into the world with nothing but one's freedom (and reason) and one must create oneself as one sees fit. On the other, the naturalistic cast of Rand's ethics suggests a view that might be thought of as having much in common with modern evolutionary theory, according to which behaviors that increase an individual's "fitness" (properly speaking, the inclusive fitness of their genes) are favored by natural selection. This biological perspective, however, is problematic for a couple of reasons. Some would argue that selection occurs at multiple levels, including those of genetic elements, individual organisms, and single-species and multi-species groups, and that group selection cannot be reduced to selection at the level of the individual. It is also very unclear how genetic propensities might manifest themselves psychologically in humans. If "increasing inclusive fitness" is some kind of evolutionary rule of thumb that lies behind, though does not determine, human behavior, it is at least possible that the rule is most effectively expressed in humans by the cultivation of certain non-egoistic reasons for acting (Wilson 1989). Thanks to James Rossie for continued discussion of these issues.

9. Although I am in agreement with Rand and Smith that one's qualities of intellect and character are not determined by the society in which one grows up, it seems highly implausible to think "[nor] are we social in the sense that our characters are shaped by others" (Smith 2006, 129). I doubt that one could develop the kind of rationality that Rand endorses (particularly the virtue of justice) without others around. Growing up in a bad society at least allows us to compare and contrast ourselves with others—to gain a sense of how we are similar and different from others around us—and to learn moral concepts, which, as we mature, we are of course free to challenge. The rationally self-sufficient man living alone on the desert

(3) Human relationships are by nature contractual. We are such as to rationally trade values with each other, according to contractual agreements.[10]

Although (1) and (2) deserve full discussion in their own right, I am most interested here in (3), which must be understood as a claim that virtuous human relationships are predominantly contractual, rather than exclusively so, owing to the prominence of love and friendship in Rand's work, brought out in Smith's appendix (287–304). Moreover, the emphasis on noncontractual relationships with others in Smith's books serves actually to undermine Rand's egoistic and individualistic view of human nature and allows for the possibility that rational action may be undertaken for the common interest and not only for one's self.

Despite the fact that Rand sometimes uses the language of contracts and trade when discussing love and friendship, it is very clear both from Rand's own writings and from Smith's treatment that true friendship cannot be reduced to an agreement to trade benefits, as I have discussed elsewhere (see Cullyer 2006). Rather it consists in the recognition of a character similar to one's own, in responding to another person because of who they are, just as for Aristotle the best kind of friendship is that based on similarity of character. The egoist may even risk her life for another. For example, Bill risks his life for the woman he loves because "for him to courageously attempt the rescue and not 'chicken out' would be in his interest (assuming that he values the woman's well-being more than his own life without her)" (Smith 2006, 194). The egoistic reason for this action is that this woman is one of the things that make Bill's life worth living. Bill is making no sacrifice, but rationally placing her well-being, which he sees as central to his own happiness, above his own safety. We should note that Smith is clear that the virtuous egoist can love others noninstrumentally, precisely because "[a]nother person might be valuable by becoming a vital ingredient of what a person's happiness consists of" (302).

---

island is only *rationally* self-sufficient if, prior to his isolation, his character and intellect have been formed by his own choices, but choices made in a social context which shapes them. For further discussion of this topic, see Cullyer 2006.

10. The claim "by nature" here does not, of course, imply that we are born able to do these things, rather that we are born with the tendencies to develop these behaviors. I am inspired to focus on (3) not only by Smith's invocation of the rational trader principle (2006, 163), but also by the following statement from Allan Gotthelf's work: "Independent, rational individuals have much to gain from living with others . . . [b]ut these benefits depend ultimately on each individual's independent choice to think and produce, and *then to trade values, material and spiritual, with others*" (Gotthelf 2000, 77, italics added for emphasis).

I would like to add here that this does not reduce the loved other to merely a part of me rather than an end in herself. For surely we are to understand that this love is mutual; though my friend and I remain separate agents our interests have interpenetrated to the extent that I become part of my friend's happiness and she part of mine. But if friendship is such a mutual affair, then we might object that human flourishing is after all a social rather than individualistic and egoistic enterprise. The virtuous "egoist" who is a good friend might well think it rational, in certain circumstances, to act for the sake not of herself, but of herself and her friend; a common interest gets substituted for the interest of the self. Now this might formally conform to egoism in two respects (teleologically, acting for the sake of "us" promotes my own happiness, and I only love those who are sufficiently similar to me that I find them valuable companions). But I suspect that most of us would agree that a friendship will not be rewarding (or be a friendship at all) if all my actions toward my friend are determined by thoughts of my long-term self-interest. I would like to suggest that the good that friends offer us is only available if one is able to act on reasons that specify "us" (or even "you"), rather than "I."[11] If I make plans for my best friend and me to go on vacation, it seems bizarre to think that the best way to make this plan would be to think of the benefits that I might get out of the vacation, rather than planning the vacation so that we will both enjoy it. This kind of "for us" reasoning is teleologically consistent with egoism, since I am acting in a way that ultimately promotes my happiness, given that maintaining and enhancing the friendship is of value to me. But if friendship is truly for Rand one of the highest goods that can make life worth living, then teleological, ethical egoism seems to be consistent with and might even require cultivation of reasons that take the form "for the sake of the common interest," or "for the sake of others" and make no reference to me as agent at the level of motivation and practical reasoning.[12] That insight may lead one to conclude that the human good is not, after all, individualistic, and that human nature is not at heart contractual.

11. Thus, we might wonder whether Bill's teleologically egoistic decision to risk his life for his lover is at the motivational level simply a judgment that it is appropriate to save his lover, rather than a complex judgment: "It is appropriate to save you, because you're part of my happiness."

12. See Nagel (1978, 132): "Reasons of a given sort continually require their own suppression. The only way to run downstairs is not to try, you cannot make her love you by doing what you think will make her love you. . . . Exclusive concern for one's long-term advantage is not to one's long-term advantage."

I think, however, that Smith would resist that conclusion for the following reason. Though the kind of love sketched above is incredibly valuable, in human relationships it is the exception and not the norm in Rand's view. Very few people are likely to be valuable to us in this way (130–32). The possibility of loving another for who he is, to the extent that that person may come to be someone whose interest becomes part of my own, and mine part of his, provides an important exception to the norm that humans rationally trade values with each other, but we can still maintain that humans are *predominantly* contractual traders. In the majority of cases, relationships with each other are based on agreements to exchange goods and services, and the deal is off when one party breaks the terms of the contract.

But in fact Smith (2006, 258–61) recognizes a multiplicity of social relationships that enhance the flourishing of the individual (for example, familial relationships, a variety of friendships and acquaintanceships, and those of fellow prisoners in a concentration camp), and which are all based on affection, respect, and shared activity. The result is, as I have argued elsewhere (Cullyer 2006), that the careful reader may wonder whether Rand's view that man is a "contractual" animal, rather than a "lone wolf" or a "social animal" (Smith 2006, 130) can any longer be sustained. Smith begins to address this worry by noting that although generosity is only rational when it represents a fair trade of one value for another, the return that the benefactor receives in compensation for his service is not necessarily material: "the return can take many forms—intellectual, emotional, the pleasure of a person's company, the deepening of a relationship" (261). One might agree with Smith here that if I give away a football ticket to an acquaintance, I am certainly acting in a way that shows the value I place on the relationship is greater than the value I place on the ticket. I gain from the act of generosity by deepening our friendship, and "trade" the ticket for something better. But the act of generosity is not truly a trade *with* my acquaintance unless I give the ticket to her with an expectation of receiving a determinate quantifiable and commensurable benefit in return. That return does not have to be a material one. It is a genuine trade if I give her the ticket, and she helps me with my homework. One can imagine a relationship based on a contractual agreement to trade such values (which Aristotle would call a friendship based on utility/advantage). But if I "trade" a football ticket *for* the deepening of a friendship, has "trade" here not become a mere metaphor? The pleasure of company and the deepening of relationships are surely benefits to be shared and enjoyed communally, not traded?[13] If this is the case, then individual human flourishing may turn out to be the activity of the individual who is fully immersed in shared activities and purposes, rather than merely the rational trading of benefits between contractual individuals. The virtuous agent may still be an egoist, formally speaking, in that she realizes that what is really in her interest is to engage in shared activities and purposes. But the "I" tends to become a "we," and the other and self united in a relationship that promotes *our* happiness.

So far we have been considering relationships with others whom we know and to whom we are partial. Although I have argued for the rationality in these situations of acting for the common interest rather than out of self-interest, Rand and Smith can still appeal to the teleological argument that acting for the common interest in these cases is always ultimately for the sake of self, and thus ultimately egoistic. But I would like to emphasize that if certain human relationships are really valuable to the self, then acting ultimately for the sake of the self may require, at the level of first-order reasoning, cultivation of non-egoistic reasons and of thinking of oneself as part of a greater whole.

However, there is one area of Smith's concern, that of rights, in which self-interest seems to drop out of the egoist's worldview even at the level of the grand teleological end. While altruism is placing others above the self as a "fundamental rule of life," egoism does not entail sacrificing others for the sake of oneself, because the true egoist recognizes an objective and impartial right of everyone to pursue their own interest (Smith 2006, 39). When discussing rights later in the book, Smith does not try to argue that recognizing and respecting the rights of others is directly or indirectly in one's self-interest (170–75). In fact, the grounding of individual rights that she delineates looks rather Kantian: "Every living human being is an end in himself, not the means to the ends or the welfare of others" (171). The respecting of others' rights, therefore, looks like it is a constraint on and exception to the egoistic ethical norm; act in self-interest *except* when it would infringe the rights of others.

13. Although I do not have room to explore the possibility here, it is likely that we should construe the concepts of "trade" and the "contractual animal" as implicitly capitalist in their connotation, given Rand's arguments for the naturalism of capitalism (*CUI*). If this is correct, then other types of barter, contract, and reciprocity in human societies would on Rand's view be either unnatural or primitive precursors of capitalist modes of exchange. There are, of course, a large number of types of reciprocal exchange possible within communities, and many of them are discussed and analyzed in Mauss 1954, a classic anthropological treatise. On the relationship between Rand's politics and her ethics, see Cullyer 2006.

Smith argues in her earlier work *Moral Rights and Political Freedom* (1995) that rights and egoism rest on the same teleological basis; since the goal of each individual is to maintain her life and to flourish, each individual requires freedom from the predatory actions of others. But the theoretical coherence of rights and egoism does not answer the following question: what is going on in the mind of the virtuous egoist when she chooses to respect the rights of others? Imagine a situation where a tyrant offers material security, protection of one's friends and family members, and the opportunity to pursue one's talents to the virtuous egoist, on the condition that she must torture perceived enemies of the state. Smith makes it very clear that the virtuous egoist would forego this opportunity, but to understand why, we have to turn to her earlier book. There, Smith rejects the Hobbesian argument that respecting the rights of others is basically a strategy for self-protection and argues instead: "ill-begotten gains such as those obtained through rights violations are not the stuff that a good life is made of" (Smith 1995, 71). Is this rationale egoistic? The virtuous egoist certainly does not think her happiness consists in violating others' rights, but although at one point Smith suggests that individuals who live free with untrammeled rights might actually be of more benefit to me than those whose rights are violated, the impression given by the use of impersonal language is that the virtuous egoist will not violate others' rights because of her commitment to the existence of rights as an impersonal good: irrespective of what benefits I may gain or lose when others' rights are respected or violated, "the world is a far richer place for the existence of free people" (Smith 1995, 73).

Let us expand upon the above thought: I, qua rational agent, cannot be happy if I violate rights, because of my rational recognition that my own rights are no more important than and do not trump those of my neighbors Bob, Carol, or David. Now Bob, Carol, David, and I, although each pursuing our individual happiness, should recognize ourselves as having a common interest, in that we are all rights-holders. Thus despite the allegedly individualistic and egoistic grounding of rights, just as true friendship is based on recognition of the similarity of one's own character to that of another, with the result that individual interests become merged into the common interest, so at a more impartial and political level, recognition of similarity of the rights claims of the self and of others should foster a sense of community where individual interests coincide to form a common interest. Now if the common interest is merely the sum of individual interests then there might appear to be no inconsistency or tension between Randian egoism and acting for the sake of the common interest. However, although Rand believes that rational self-interests cannot conflict, she does not think that I should care about the interests of others as much my own. So the virtuous egoist will not infringe the rights of Bill, Carol, and David. But if someone imprisons Carol and David (because they have red hair, while I'm a blonde), it is not necessarily rational for me, or Bill, to do anything about it, if Carol and David are not people who offer any particular value to Bill and to me. An appeal to the "common interest" ("the suffering of Carol and David hurts us all") may not be effective, because it is only rational to care about my own interest, and Carol and David's suffering does not really impact me in any way. Although Smith argues that the virtuous egoist will, for the most part, not sanction evil by tacit approval of it, she also stresses that when the egoist speaks out against evil she will do so only on the condition that it would serve her own long-term advantage (Smith 2006, 162–63).[14]

When considering these issues in Rand and Smith, I run into a problem. What exactly do they mean by "acting for one's long-term rational interest"? On one hand, it seems to me that acting in this way is conceived of by Rand as what we may call a "rational maximizer" model of egoism: the virtuous egoist is not crudely thinking about how she can maximize material goods or pleasure for herself, rather she's thinking about all the values (psychological, spiritual, artistic, and material) that enhance her life qua human individual. Her long-term self-interest will be rationally maximized both by the activities that she undertakes alone, and by a combination of competitive and cooperative strategies, trade being the most important and frequent, that serve to create and enhance values for her.[15]

However, the virtuous egoist's respect for rights and propensity for genuine friendship suggest a nonmaximizing rational self model of egoism: she may believe at the reflective level that her happiness consists in

14. I use "evil" here in the restrictive sense of "evil" used by Smith (2006, 160), manifestations of which seem to be violations of basic human rights. On the issue of when to speak out against evil, Smith says: "When speaking would be a sacrifice, the surrender of a greater value for the sake of a lesser value, a person should not speak. When *not* speaking would be a sacrifice, however, as it would be when a more fully considered perspective reveals that a person's long-range flourishing would be jeopardized by his silence, he must" (162–63).

15. In addition to trade, one might think of the various competitive and cooperative strategies that can be modeled using game theory (Dawkins 1976).

rational activity, but may think of rational activity as constituted by acting: (1) for the sake of maintaining and enhancing one's own life; but also
(2) for sake of the common interest. (2) is grounded in the agent's judgment that others are similar to her, and share interests with her, both at
the partial level of friendships, and at the impartial level of rights-holders
in the political community. Let us call this the "rational nonmaximizer"
model of egoism, which some would likely be loath to call a form of egoism at all and would instead call a form of self-love that can accommodate
non-egoistic reasons for acting.[16]

   We can use an example from Smith's book to illustrate the difference
here between the "rational maximizer" and "rational nonmaximizer"
models. It might, claims Smith, be in the self-interest of the virtuous egoist to help Jews escape from Nazi Germany, although the agent is herself a
Gentile (2006, 254–55). This is an interesting example, because it is an example of heroic conduct that seems very hard to explain as egoistic. Smith
does not explain how this could be a self-interested action, but using the
two models of egoism, we can suggest some possible answers.

   On one hand, using the "rational maximizer" model, one might argue that this would be the virtuous thing to do if the egoist has reason
to think that Nazi policies may in the future threaten him.[17] A different
suggestion is that the actions of the Nazis might be thought to be so evil
and destructive that they actually threaten the very cooperative mech-
anisms of society that make the egoist's own rational self-maintenance
possible. However, using the "rational nonmaximizer" model, one could
argue that the rational individual simply cannot be happy if she lets the
rights-violating slaughter and torture of individuals in her community
continue because she (rationally) thinks of individual rights as equal, and
of victims of the Nazis as similar (in their rights) to herself. The "common interest" of all those who possess rights has a pull on her, even when
her own rights are not in jeopardy and even when she may risk much
personally to aid others.[18] This is a type of egoism only if we are willing
to concede that self-interest and thoughts about one's own happiness at a

16. See, for example, Harry Frankfurt's account of self-love (Frankfurt 2004, 69–100).

17. This sort of reasoning is suggested by Smith: "a person's failure to oppose evil exposes him to the damage to values that others' evil threatens" (160).

18. She will also surely think of the Nazis as grossly undeserving of any tacit approval,
owing to their rights violations. This is suggested by Smith herself when she writes that the
refusal to sanction evil "bestows on the grossly undeserving the spiritual shelter of the sanc-
tioner's tacit approval, for that is the message that his failure to condemn conveys" (Smith
2006, 160).

reflective level are consistent with practical reasoning, which can take as a primary goal the preservation of the interests of others.[19]

I raise these issues to highlight what I take to be a puzzle in Rand's ethics and in sophisticated versions of egoism more generally. On one hand, the virtuous egoist is conceived of as a rational trader and creator of values for himself; his actions are always designed to promote his own long-term self-interest. While it is not the case that he will not help others, he will only help others for his own sake. He is a maximizer. On the other hand, the virtuous egoist is able to recognize the similarity between himself and others both at the partial (friends) and impartial (rights-holders) levels, and thus to conceive of interests that transcend the self and of interests that are shared; and of oneself as part of a greater whole, a "we." That's what it means to be "egoistically" committed to one's rational self as a nonmaximizer. According to the latter model, while it is rational to maintain one's own life and enhance it, it is also rational to see that others are similar to oneself, that we have common interests, and that we trade and share. Happiness on this model is ultimately to meet the claims of the self while recognizing the similar claims of others, proudly, and with independence and integrity. At times, Smith's treatment of Rand's ethics actually gives us reason to think that the "rational nonmaximizer" view is a plausible one, and perhaps that's because Rand herself is caught between these two rather different models of "egoism."

19. It has been claimed that an agent could be acting both egoistically and altruistically at the same time (Badhwar 1993). The argument is that altruistic action is motivated in part by an agent's interest in affirming his altruistic dispositions as central to himself. Although I am in sympathy with this line of thinking, it is not clear that either egoism or altruism are the right terms to use with reference to what Badhwar is describing. Rather one might think in terms of acting for the sake of common interest, of the ability to see the similarity between the self and others, and of a conception of a self who acts for the sake of the common interest. In fact what I term the "rational nonmaximizer" model of egoism seems to transcend the egoism/altruism dichotomy to such an extent that it may lead one to question whether egoism and altruism are the right terms to use when thinking about ethics.

Egoistic Relations with Others
Response to Cullyer

TARA SMITH

elen Cullyer is concerned about the professed egoism of Rand's ethics standing alongside its recognition of rights and of ideal friendships in which self-interest comes to be "transcended" by concern for the friends' "common interest." In this way, Cullyer seemingly reveals a conflict between "maximizer" and "nonmaximizer" models of egoism. I don't think this conflict is genuine, however. It depends on an incomplete understanding—for which I may be partially responsible—of Rand's rationale for respecting rights and of her view of the value of friendship. I'm going to try to clarify both, spending most of my time on the latter.

Value in the Egoist's Relationships with Others

Does Rand's recognition of ideal friendships compromise the egoism of her ethics? Cullyer contends that Rand's account of proper relations with others "allows for the possibility that rational action may be undertaken for the common interest and not only for one's self." Because friendship is to friends' mutual benefit, Cullyer concludes that human flourishing is social after all, "rather than an . . . egoistic enterprise."

Notice that this pits the social *versus* the egoistic. In fact, the two are not opposites or contraries, however. Something can be pursued for the sake of my interest (i.e., egoistically) without the fact that it serves my interest excluding its bringing benefits to other people. For Rand, in a friendship, the "common interest" is a proper end only to the extent that it serves the agent's interest. That an interest is shared, or common to two people, does not render it no longer in my interest.

Cullyer seems to suppose that it is necessary to submerge my interest in order to advance your interest or "our" interest. Yet in truth, "our interest" consists of our individual interests, in the context set by the value that each of us finds in the other and in our friendship. Once I value these things, "my self-interest" no longer refers to the exact same list of things that it did before I acquired these values.

Cullyer writes that the virtuous egoist sometimes finds it rational "to act for the sake not of herself, but of herself and her friend; a common interest gets substituted for the interest of the self." But on Rand's view, the common interest is not "substituted" for an individual's self-interest. The reason I care about the package "my friend *and* myself" is that I care about my well-being. This does not mean that I don't care about my friend. The reason I do care about him is his great value in enhancing my life. But I have reason to act for the sake of that package of interests (mine and his) because our well-being enhances my well-being. Rand can agree that a "we" develops and that "our happiness" becomes meaningful, but this is not "our" happiness as *opposed* to "my" happiness. Rather, this particular "our," I come to realize, is the best way of promoting "my."

Cullyer concedes that Rand's view might be "formally" egoistic, but contends that "a friendship will not be rewarding (or be a friendship at all) if all my actions toward my friend are determined by thoughts of my long-term self-interest." I think this frames the issue in a misleading way, however. For it contains a crucial ambiguity. The phrasing—"*all* my actions" determined by thoughts of "*my* self-interest" (emphases added)— suggests that the thoughts are of my self-interest *narrowly construed*, such that my self-interest excludes anyone else's (including "ours"). If that's the meaning, then I agree: that isn't true friendship. But another sensible reading is available, one that is compatible with both true friendship and egoism, namely: My actions in the friendship *are* determined by thoughts of my self-interest, in that those thoughts governed my developing our friendship in the first place. It was egoistic values that led me to conclude that you add value to my life, and on those grounds, to cultivate this relationship. As you have become a value to me, you have become a part of my life and my well-being.

It's helpful here to bear in mind the naturalistic roots of all value, for Rand. Life is a series of actions. Rand observes that human beings can survive only by making those actions life-sustaining—i.e., by acting to achieve objective (life-furthering) values. But because life *is* a series of actions, the values that sustain a life themselves constitute that life. My values are the things at which my actions aim. My life depends on and consists of the achievement of values. Thus, while you exist as a separate entity external to me, insofar as you are my friend—a value to me—your well-being is part of my well-being. And in considering your well-being when choosing my actions (as a good friend would), I am still acting for my self-interest. (Indeed, this is what it means to say that my friend's well-being becomes part of my own.)

(Parenthetically, I hope all this helps us to see why Cullyer's vacation example misses its mark. It treats the other person as at once a friend and not a friend. That is, it *would* be ridiculous for me, if I do value you and our relationship, to plan a joint vacation as if I didn't value those things. The example relies, in other words, on dropping the context, ignoring the relevant fact that you are a *friend* and that ours is a relationship that is an important value to me.)

My point, then, is that Rand's view is not merely "formally" egoistic, but substantively egoistic, since the reason for nurturing the friend and the friendship is their value to me. When it does make sense for an egoist to act for the sake of "common interest" in a friendship, he is not recognizing additional types of reasons for acting, besides egoistic ones.

A last word on this issue: Cullyer raises some interesting questions about Rand's "trade" and "contract" language. In speculating that I would view ideal friendships as rare and thus stand by Rand's view of man as "predominantly" contractual, Cullyer reveals what I think is too legalistic a sense of "contract." She sees ideal friendship as an alternative to the contractual model. But I don't think that Rand does. Ideal friendships, too, are trades in the very familiar sense that values are gained by both parties. In characterizing man as a contractual animal, Rand does not mean that all our social relations are governed by written agreements, the sort certified by a notary public, legally enforceable—or even, by less formal prior arrangements, of the "If you help me with the homework, I'll water your plants" sort. Metaphorical or not, what "contract" and "trade" bring out is reciprocity—the fact that an exchange of values takes place—values coming to each person from the other. I don't think the fact that many values in a friendship are enjoyed "communally," as Cullyer emphasizes, means that a trade isn't taking place. We each gain benefits and some of them are shared; we *both* gain those (see Smith 2006, appendix; Smith 2005). Insofar as they are benefits made possible by the partnership or collaboration that a friendship is, however, they are benefits that each of the friends gains as a result, at least in part, of the other person's contribution.

Respect for Rights

Let's turn, more briefly, to the other stance that strikes Cullyer as contradicting Rand's egoism: her recognition of individual rights. Cullyer takes rights to be constraints that inhibit an individual's pursuit of his interest. Respecting rights, Cullyer writes, thus looks like an "exception to the egoistic ethical norm."

Here, unfortunately, I think that Cullyer has misunderstood Rand's reasons for recognizing rights. In my 2006 work, I explain that Rand rejects a policy of sacrificing others to oneself "in part, on grounds of consistency," and Cullyer refers to this.[1] What I proceed to say immediately following that, however, is: "*More fundamentally,* Rand rejects predation on the egoistic grounds that such a policy would not truly serve a person's interest" (Smith 2006, 39, emphasis added; see also 170). And in my earlier book on rights to which Cullyer refers, I don't merely "suggest" that living among others who are free might be of more benefit to me than the alternatives; I argue that quite plainly. To quote myself: "it is in an individual's *personal interest* to respect others' freedom. By respecting others' rights, a person is preserving the conditions in which *she is most likely to gain* by exchange with others" (Smith 1995, 73, emphasis added; see also 69–73).

Rand's basic idea is that man can only achieve objective values through rational action and he can only engage in rational action when free of others' initiation of physical force. Freedom is the condition necessary for any genuine values to be gained by human beings. It is in my interest that other people create and enjoy values, for that deepens the pool of material and spiritual values—be they physical goods, knowledge, art, inspiration, etc.—that people have to offer one another. Correspondingly, it is in my interest that others be in conditions under which such creation of values is possible. Therefore, I, as an egoist, should make it a principle to respect others' freedom.

Thus, when I wrote, "the world is a far richer place for the existence

1. I cite Rand's observation that if a man claims to have "a case for his right to self-interest, then he must concede that the ground on which he claims the right to self-interest also applies to every other human being" (qtd. in Smith 2006, 39).

of free people," as Cullyer quotes me, I did not mean that this is an *inherently* good thing. Rather, I meant that the world is thereby a richer environment, more stocked with value from which I stand to benefit. So, without time to go into more depth on the case for rights—it's the subject of another book—I do want to make clear that Rand's recognition of rights is an application of rational egoism to a particular aspect of social relations, not a contradiction of it.[2]

2. It is also worth noting, vis-à-vis Cullyer's example of the tyrant offering material security to a person who agrees to torture "perceived enemies of the state," that Rand held that "morality ends where a gun begins." I explain this important condition in Smith 2006, 94–95. For further elaboration, see *Atlas* 1023–24; "What is Capitalism?" *CUI* 8, 15–16; and *Q&A* 114.

Virtuous Egoism and Virtuous Altruism

CHRISTINE SWANTON

Thinkers such as Nietzsche and Ayn Rand receive bad press because they either appear to advocate (in Nietzsche's case) or in fact explicitly advocate, egoism as an ideal of conduct. Nietzsche has been somewhat rehabilitated, and Tara Smith is attempting to do the same for Rand. In both cases the instrument, or at least one important instrument, for rehabilitation is virtue ethics. Does this use contaminate virtue ethics, or does it improve understanding of both Nietzsche and Rand, and of moral theory generally? I firmly believe the latter is the case. While improving understanding of Rand in this way may be difficult, Smith does a great job of applying virtue ethics to accomplish this task. She shows that a virtue ethical understanding of both egoism and altruism provides the needed shift in our thinking and enables us to understand the idea of the *virtuous* egoist. I would like to add to that understanding a conception of the virtuous altruist, for not all altruism is virtuous.

Why does Rand advocate egoism as opposed to virtuous altruism? The question is a pressing one, for Smith rightly claims, "[b]ecause altruism calls for the sacrifice of self to others, people frequently assume that egoism must call for the sacrifice of others to oneself. Rand explicitly rejects this view. . . . More fundamentally, Rand rejects predation on the egoistic grounds that such a policy would not truly serve a person's interests" (Smith 2006, 39). One might think then that virtuous egoism is nonpredatory and virtuous altruism is not inappropriately self-sacrificing, so virtuous egoism and virtuous altruism are two sides of the same coin. Why then does Rand want to call herself an egoist? Smith answers:

> E. J. Bond characterizes altruism as the policy of "always denying oneself for the sake of others." Burton Potter presents altruism as "the position that one should always act for the welfare of others." . . . Lawrence Blum observes that in its most prevalent usage, altruism refers to placing the interests of others ahead of one's own. This is clearly how Rand understands altruism. She describes it as the thesis that self sacrifice is a person's highest moral duty. . . . Peikoff stresses that altruism is not a synonym for kindness, generosity, or good will, but the "doctrine that man should place others above self as the fundamental rule of life." (Smith 2006, 38–39)

These definitions are not exactly equivalent, but I assume the kind of altruism rejected should be understood thus:

> (A) Whenever there is an opportunity to benefit someone, one must do so even when that constitutes personal sacrifice.

A "sacrifice" occurs in Rand's sense when one surrenders something of greater (objective) value to oneself for something of lesser value to oneself (Smith 2006, 39, citing *VOS* 50).

I do not know of anyone who subscribes to this kind of altruism (A), which, in fact, violates Kant's doctrine of everyone having equal worth. If egoism is defined in terms of the negation of (A), then clearly egoism is the normatively acceptable principle of conduct, though it would give precious little action guidance. Surely, one might think, Rand is an egoist in a stronger sense. It would seem so. According to Smith, for Rand, egoism is "the paramount commitment to one's own well-being" (2006, 24). She also states: "More precisely, it is the view that each person's primary moral obligation is to achieve his own well-being and he should not sacrifice his well-being for the well-being of others" (23).

It seems that we are to suppose that Rand is an egoist in the following sense:

(E) One must never benefit someone else if that constitutes personal sacrifice.

At first sight, (E), extreme egoism, seems as extreme a position as (A), and surely, one might think, common sense and decency would reject both. Thus, one might suppose that (E) should be replaced by:

(VE) One should not benefit another if that constitutes nonvirtuous personal sacrifice.

Virtuous egoism, (VE), might also seem incompatible with (E), and one might think that Ayn Rand's egoism should be replaced by (VE). However, Smith's title, *Ayn Rand's Normative Ethics: The Virtuous Egoist*, should give us pause. The way I read Tara Smith on Rand is to portray Rand as believing that (E), properly understood, is compatible with (VE). This dramatic connection between (E) and (VE) is effected by two important moves. These are:

(i)   Since what constitutes one's interests or well-being is determined by objective values, one's own beliefs and desires do not necessarily determine what is in one's interests.

(ii) Since what counts as an objective value is determined in part by virtue concepts (e.g., honesty, integrity, virtuous productivity, and justice), what counts as something being in one's interests is determined at least in part by virtue, and what counts as a genuine sacrifice to one's interests or well-being is determined at least in part by virtue. For example, pain suffered in the cause of virtuous productivity is not a sacrifice; it is not against one's interests to have failed to secure a job that one has not deserved. Hence it is not a *sacrifice* to forego forwarding a fake CV in order to con people into thinking one deserves a job.[1]

Given (i) and (ii), one can read (E) in terms of (VE): One should not benefit another if that constitutes a *genuine* personal sacrifice, i.e., a nonvirtuous personal sacrifice. The claim that, for Rand, (E) should be read as (VE) is discussed in the next section. There remains the problem of the relation between (VE) and virtuous altruism, and how Smith conceives of

---

1. I am not claiming here that no virtuous behavior is a sacrifice, or that Rand would claim this. All that is necessary for (ii) is that not all apparent "costs" undergone virtuously are (genuine) sacrifices to a virtuous agent.

Rand's conception of the latter. Discussion of Smith's Rand and virtuous altruism is the topic of the final section.

Virtuous Egoism

I have claimed that according to Smith's Rand, (E) should be read as (VE), and this claim is justified by understanding well-being as constituted at least in part, by virtue. To say that personal well-being or happiness is constituted at least in part by virtue is an idea familiar from eudaimonistic virtue ethics. Smith, in places, appears to suggest that the connection between virtue and well-being is purely instrumental. She says, in her discussion of the "master virtue" rationality, "[i]f a person seeks his own life and happiness, rationality is the essential means to success" (2006, 56). Again, in explicating Rand's claim that "honesty is a profoundly selfish virtue," Smith claims that the value of honesty is to be found most profoundly not in the damage done to the reputation and social relations of the dishonest person, but in the individual's relation to reality in general. Facing facts, seeking knowledge, and avoiding all kinds of faking are all necessary for proper interaction with reality. Honesty, in short, goes hand in hand with courage. The value of honesty, too, seems to be instrumental, but in a deep way.

However, it is not clear that all the virtues are to be understood as having instrumental value. In discussing independence, Rand observes, a person faces a basic choice: whether to survive by the "work of his own mind or as a parasite fed by the mind of others" (Smith 2006, 113). Is independence, understood thus, a merely instrumental value? Or is Rand claiming that there is something ignoble about being a parasite—that, in other words, being a parasite is not in one's genuine interests because it is dishonorable, demeaning, and so forth? If this is indeed what she is saying, then for her, what is in one's interests has an important aretaic component. However, Smith claims on behalf of Rand that "the central argument for independence" is that it is "vital to all rational thought and action and thereby vital to human survival" (2006, 119). Being a second-hander goes against the idea of the good as "*an evaluation* of facts of reality by man's consciousness according to a rational standard of value" (Smith 2006, 119, citing *CUI* 14). Therefore, "Nothing can be objectively valuable to a person without that person's independent assessment of it" (119). In other words, given that rationality has instrumental value, so does independence.

One might be tempted to think that, insofar as virtue is only instru-

mentally necessary for an individual's well-being, if the connection between virtue and well-being were to fail, Rand's egoism would cease to
demand virtue, and (E) would be as unattractive a position as it appears
on the surface to be. But this thought would be a mistake. For Smith's
reading of Rand shows the connection between virtue and well-being
to be so fundamental to human existence for Rand that the connection
would fail only if there were extremely dramatic changes in human nature and the conditions of human life. Indeed as Smith herself suggests,
this deep connection makes the distinction between virtue as a mere
means to well-being and being partly constitutive of it itself problematic.

This claim is controversial as a reading of Rand, and I now need to
justify it and my reading of Smith. It will be objected by David Kelley
(2001) and others that though for Rand what is in one's interests is determined by objective values, so (i) above is true, it is not the case that what
is in one's interests is aretaic, so (ii) above is false. According to Kelley, on
Rand's view value is independent of virtue: "Virtue is a derivative aspect
of flourishing in the sense that what counts as a virtuous action, policy,
or trait of character depends on prior assumptions about what things are
valuable" (Kelley 2001, 69).

However, my claim does not depend on a rejection of this thesis
about the relation between value and virtue, properly understood. Value
(or rather what is valuable, i.e., what things are worthy of preservation,
creation, appreciation, maintenance, pursuit) is for sure not *reducible* to
virtue.[2] Living things for example, or at least a class of living things (such
as ancient kauri trees) have value regardless of whether they themselves
have virtue or are handled or regarded virtuously. But it does not follow from this that value can be understood *entirely* nonaretaically. Rand
would agree with Aristotle that pleasure as such is not an objective value:
what has objective value is pleasure that is excellent or good. That is, valuable pleasure is pleasure that is proper to human beings and not human
beings who are gluttons, wanton, and so on. The same point applies to
friendship and a whole host of other so called "values." As Smith claims:
"The standard of value is life *qua* man or a flourishing life . . . because
man can only survive by respecting the requirements of his distinctive

2. This general conception of value is compatible with what I take to be Rand's response-
dependent concept of value and of attributes generally. See Gotthelf (2000, 57): a (perceivable)
attribute is an "object's being of such a nature that it will be perceived by humans in this form
and by the extraterrestrials in that form." Similarly, values are values for entities of a certain
type.

nature" (2006, 30). And survival qua man is not just mere physical survival. It is "complete physical and spiritual well-being. . . . Spiritual values include such things as intelligence, self respect, art, friendship, a rewarding career" (32). Notice however that, as just suggested, friendship, for example, can only be regarded as a "spiritual value" if it satisfies at least some canons of virtue. Friendship incompatible with self-respect, for example, does not.

I am not disagreeing with the Randian thesis that survival proper to human beings as beings with certain complex capacities and needs existing in certain sorts of worlds provides the ultimate grounds for standards of excellence. But the notion of "proper" to human beings is highly normative, depending on conceptions of self-realization. Such conceptions, in turn, depend on all kinds of theories of human nature, many of which are controversial. I here assume that what Badhwar (2001) calls a bleak but long life is not a self-realized life; it is not for Rand a life *proper* to human beings. As Smith puts it, it is not survival qua man, for it neglects his "spiritual" nature.

I conclude, then, that according to Smith's Rand, (E) is to be read as (VE). For what counts as something's being in one's interests is determined in part by virtue, so what counts as a genuine sacrifice is determined also by virtue. Pain suffered in the cause of virtuous productivity is not a sacrifice; it is not against one's interests to have failed to secure a job which one has not deserved.

Virtuous Altruism

There remains a problem. One might think that (VE) is true only if it is compatible with virtuous altruism. Virtuous altruism (VA) may be defined as:

> (VA) One should benefit another if and only if that is virtuous (that is, instantiates a virtue such as generosity, kindness, friendship, parental virtue, and so forth), or is at least compatible with virtue.

If one's conception of virtuous egoism is incompatible with there being a virtuous form of altruism then surely that conception of (VE) is flawed. However, Smith (2006, chap. 10) argues that Rand does allow for generosity and kindness, for example, properly understood as virtues. The issue to be addressed in this section is whether Smith's Randian conception of these virtues, and thereby of (VA), is acceptable. To begin, we must investigate how, according to Smith's understanding of Rand, Rand can have a conception of (VA) which can be understood as compatible with (VE).

Rand claims that at the heart of a virtue of generosity is integrity. For generosity to be virtuous, the "giving more than the recipient has the right to expect or demand" (Smith 2006, 257) must express the agent's integrity. What is generosity that expresses integrity? Integrity is "loyalty to one's convictions and values; it is the policy of acting in accordance with one's values, of expressing, upholding and translating them into practical reality" (176, citing *VOS* 52–53). So giving more than the recipient has the right to expect or demand is a virtuous expression of generosity only if it expresses or is at least compatible with, the agent's integrity. Remember, too, that one's values, to be genuine values, must be objective; they are not determined by an agent's actual desires, emotions, or beliefs. It seems that we have a concept of virtuous altruism. But it is still unclear how it can be compatible with (VE). Smith explains with the help of an example: "We can easily imagine the teacher being generous with his time, staying beyond the scheduled sessions to work with the student, without its being a sacrifice. If he greatly values the student's development and giving his best possible performance and if he can spare the resources on a given afternoon to go overtime, it can be in his interest to give the student more attention than the student could reasonably demand or expect" (Smith 2006, 258).

In other words, generosity is not a sacrifice other things being equal, if you have a stake in the interests of the beneficiary. You have a stake in someone else's interests if, for example, you love that person or value his success or well-being. It is also consistent with Rand's position that helping others may be part of one's productivity (a productivity that must express or be compatible with, integrity, pride, honesty, justice, and so on). So it appears that, for Rand, virtuous altruism may be compatible with (E) (for it may not be a [genuine] sacrifice), and in particular (VE) is compatible with Rand's conception of (VA).

Now that this is established we can address the question of whether Rand's conception of (VA) is acceptable. At the core of Rand's conception of (VA), emphasized by Smith, is the rejection of the thesis that need alone may create moral demands. This may sound heartless, but it should be remembered that the rejection of this thesis lies also at the heart of Williams's integrity objection to utilitarianism (Smart and Williams 1973, 99–117). Williams's objection is not fundamentally an objection to the maximizing or even consequentialist features of utilitarianism, but to the very idea that one's legitimate and productive projects could at any time be derailed by the needs of others, even where those needs are created by their feckless or otherwise nonvirtuous behavior.

I do not think that it is an objection to Rand that she rejects the thesis that need alone can create moral demands on a person who is in a position to satisfy them. However, one may reject this thesis, accept that people should pursue their own creative and productive projects, and yet claim that a person's concerns are too narrowly focused on herself. Is there any room in Rand, as portrayed by Smith, to criticize a person for having an excessively narrow conception of persons in whose interests she has some kind of stake? Of course the ability to be criticized in such a way would not be crudely quantitative: a woman struggling to look after her own children should not be criticized because her objective values do not include the interests of a large range of others. Before considering whether Rand is vulnerable to this criticism, we should note that if injustice is at the basis of your failure to include others in your sphere of concern because you are racist, for example, or if you are leading a shallow, unproductive life dominated by hedonism, you are most certainly criticizable for Rand: she has a basis of criticism for what we would term selfish people. But is there something missing from Rand's version of altruism? To find out, we need a deeper understanding of altruism.

Given that (A), extreme altruism, is to be rejected, how should we understand the notion of altruism? There are many senses in the psychological literature. We shall consider which, if any, are acceptable to Rand on Smith's understanding.

Sense 1. Altruism is acting "in such a way as to increase another entity's welfare at the expense of its own" (Dawkins 1976, 4).

Sense 2. Altruism is acting in such a way as to increase another's welfare at the expense of one's own, believing that cost to self is certain or likely.

Sense 3. Altruism is "a motivational state with the ultimate goal of increasing another's welfare" (Batson 1991, 6).

Sense 3a. Altruism is a motivational state with the ultimate goal of increasing another's welfare in the belief that it would be at one's own expense.

Sense 4. Altruism is a motivational state to increase another's welfare but possibly with a desire for external reward or to avoid external punishment (Davis 1996, 127–28).

Sense 4a. As above, but in the belief that it would be at one's own expense.

Sense 5. As above, but possibly with a desire to avoid internal sanctions such as guilt, empathic distress even if not by desire for external rewards or punishments—"the dominant view for some time has been that all helping acts are fundamentally egoistic" (Davis 1996, 128).

Sense 5a. As above, but in the belief that it would be at one's own expense.

Rand is clearly not opposed to behavior that increases others' welfare at personal cost (sense 1), where the notion of cost is distinguished from her notion of sacrifice. Poverty is clearly a cost to Roark in the pursuit of his productive goals, even if it is not a genuine sacrifice, in Rand's sense. However, would not Rand object to altruistic behavior where one's ultimate goal is another's welfare (sense 3)? Surely not—in helping the student in Smith's example, the teacher's ultimate goal is not the teacher's own welfare but the success of the student.

Admittedly, the waters are muddied by Rand's apparent suggestion that all altruistic motivation is ultimately "selfish": "If the person to be saved is . . . the man or woman one loves, then one can be willing to give one's own life to save him or her—for the selfish reason that life without the loved person could be unbearable" (*VOS* 52).

This brings to mind sense 4, where altruistic motivation is seen as ultimately selfish, but this is not the reading that I see in Smith. Self-regarding motivations (avoiding pangs of conscience, desire for external reward, and so on) are not exactly noble motives for altruistic behavior, and in the standard virtue ethical tradition these motivations are not marks of full virtue, and therefore not marks of fully virtuous altruism.

It seems then that though Rand rejects (A), what I have called extreme altruism, her views are compatible with several standard senses of altruism. So where is the problem? The problem lies in her conception of virtuous altruism. Although I have conceded that she has the tools for criticizing certain sorts of shallow, hedonistic, selfish lives, she lacks the resources for criticizing others who have an excessively narrow conception of interests in which they have a stake.

To show this, let us consider the famous example of Kant's unsympathetic moralist which deserves quotation in full:

> Still further: if nature had put little sympathy in the heart of this or that man; if (in other respects an honest man) he is by temperament cold and indifferent to the sufferings of others, perhaps because he himself is provided with the special gift of patience and endurance toward his own sufferings and presupposes the same in every other or even requires it; if nature had not properly fashioned such a man (who would in truth not be its worst product) for a philanthropist, would he not still find within himself a source from which to give himself a far higher worth than what a mere good-natured temperament might have? By all means! It is just then that the worth of character comes out, which is moral and incomparably the highest, namely that he is beneficent not from inclination but from duty. (*Groundwork*, Ak. 398–99 [Kant 1998])

Both Kant and virtue ethicists have resources for defending a claim that, notwithstanding the unsympathetic moralist's excessively narrow conception of those in whose interests he has a stake, he ought nonetheless to be appropriately benevolent to others with whom he has no sympathy. Rand, as far as I can see, has no such resources. Virtue ethics in general can claim that the unsympathetic moralist lacks (full) virtue because he is flawed affectively, specifically in his capacity for empathy. Appeal to the psychology of empathy can show how this is so. I digress to give a very brief account of that psychology.

One must distinguish between three types of empathy:

(i) empathy as an innate capacity;

(ii) empathy as a stable dispositional characteristic;

(iii) empathy as it occurs in specific situations (Davis, 23).

There are three corresponding types of explanation of empathic behavior:

(i) "Explanations focusing on the inherent human capacity for empathic responding must address the functional nature of such capacities; in short, why would such capacities evolve in humans at all?" (Davis 1996, 23–24).

(ii) Explanations focusing on (ii) "must address the factors which contribute to individuals' stable likelihood of utilizing the capacities they possess" (Davis 1996, 24). That is, they explain how the inherent capacity develops into a disposition. There are two primary contributors to that development: "inherited propensities" and "socialization experiences."

(iii) "[E]xplanations focusing on empathy as it occurs within specific situations must examine features of both the particular setting and of the individuals involved" (Davis 1996, 23–24).

From the perspective of virtue ethics, focus will be on (ii): individuals with defective dispositions will tend to be defective in their responses in specific situations.

There are different views about what prompts an individual to empathy and thereby to altruism. According to Hoffman's "prompting view," empathy "is uniquely well suited for bridging the gap between egoism and altruism since it can transform another person's misfortune into one's own distress, which in turn can usually be best alleviated by helping that person" (Hoffman 1978, 333, cited in Davis 1996, 29; see also Batson et al. 1981).

This view appears to support senses 5 and 5a of altruism. However, there is a problem with Hoffman's account. Tendencies to experience such distress, especially when socialized by religions that valorize self-sacrifice, have been criticized by thinkers such as Nietzsche. The point is not necessarily that such empathetic emotional reactions are inherently bad, but they can be formative of and constitutive of vice, as illustrated by Nietzsche's "pity." What is Ayn Rand's position on such emotional promptings of altruism? Is all such empathy to be deplored? Or is it deplorable only when taken to excess?

Another concept of the psychology of empathy is the empathy-altruism path posited by Batson (1991). On this view, the empathic individual adopts the target's perspective and imagines the target's thoughts and feelings. This produces feelings of compassion and tenderness labelled "empathic concern" (Davis 1996, 134). How does this relate to Batson's "prompting view": the idea that the other's distress is transformed into one's own? It looks as if Batson's model fits with senses 3 and 3a of altruism, and would be acceptable to standard virtue ethical conceptions of virtuous altruism, whereas Hoffman's is vulnerable to Nietzschean critique, and appears to render altruistic motivation ultimately egoistic. One is altruistic to alleviate the pain of feeling another's distress (senses 5 and 5a).

Classical virtue ethics is able to take advantage of psychological findings in attachment theory, empathy theory, and the like to show that an inability to have a stake in relevant others' interests may constitute deficiency in affective states and a lack of virtue. A person without such deficiencies is able to be altruistic for the sake of those in whose interests she has an interest, and those in whose interests she has an interest form a suitably broad class. Let us assume that, notwithstanding the previously quoted passage from *VOS*, Rand does not believe that all empathy is ultimately egoistic, for altruism can be motivated by concern for another's interests only. Nonetheless, Rand appears to lack the resources for criticizing people who, like Kant's unsympathetic moralist, lack empathy, but who, unlike Kant's unsympathetic moralist, are not benevolent toward those with whom he lacks empathy. Certainly for Rand, one must be just and honest toward such a person, but there appears to be no rational reason for one to be benevolent. She cannot appeal to deficiencies in the unsympathetic agent's affective state as a ground for attributing to him lack of virtue. Nor of course can she make the moves Kant makes in the *Doctrine of Virtue* for the rational status of the maxim of benevolence, and the rationality of the naturally unsympathetic person's altruism.

I conclude that Smith's Rand allows for altruistic virtue, but that the concept of such virtue has something missing. Smith's Rand, it appears to me, is unable to criticize a lack of benevolence (understood as altruism in senses 3 and 3a, where an agent helps another for the sake of the other) in an unsympathetic individual. However, Smith's book constitutes a much-needed tonic in modern substantive moral theory. The assumption that ethics is by definition other-regarding, and only concerned with (contractualist) conceptions of justice and benevolence has been dealt, fortunately, a severe blow. In particular, the highlighting of pride and productivity as ethical virtues is a much-needed achievement.

On Altruism, and on the Role of Virtues in Rand's Egoism
Response to Swanton

TARA SMITH

Swanton believes that Rand's ethics cannot be hastily dismissed, thanks to its altruism and insistence on virtue. Nonetheless, the *way* in which it upholds virtue—by maintaining that a person should pursue what is "proper" to human beings—is normatively loaded. Worse, Swanton contends, Rand's theory does not provide any reason for a person to act as if he or she values another person if, in fact, he or she does not value that person. Thus even Rand's virtuous egoist seems too "narrow" in his concerns, too stingy.

While I very much welcome the spirit in which Swanton is reading Rand, I don't think that she has captured Rand's actual view. Rand is not embracing any form of altruism, and the virtue of her virtuous egoist does not constrain his egoism. To clarify this, I'm going to take up three issues, being very brief on each: the meaning of altruism, the relationship between value and virtue, and the charge of insufficient concern for others.

The Meaning of Altruism

Although I cite several philosophers on the meaning of altruism, Swanton objects that few people actually use the term in that extreme a way.

She recommends, in effect, that we think of altruism more loosely and then try to determine which exact degree of altruism is morally proper. I don't think this approach is tenable, however, because it obscures the self-sacrificial heart of altruism by mingling it with benevolence, kindness, generosity, and charity, which seem to have softer edges and more "sensible" profiles. The problem is that while these words capture those distinct phenomena, we also need a term to identify the particular policy of placing others first, which is what the word "altruism" was coined to do, and does. Altruism, from the French "autrui," or "others," could be thought of as "other-ism"; it is a word that signifies overriding devotion to others, while "benevolence," "generosity," etc., do not. While many might balk at the idea that a person must do what he can to benefit another whenever he has the opportunity, the belief that morality demands sacrifice for others is thoroughly familiar and widely accepted. Why is Mother Teresa seen as a saint, as the model by which many people feel they should judge their own actions? Why do the writings of Peter Singer induce such discomfort and guilt? Why are campaigns to volunteer service and "give back" to the community nearly universally applauded? Because such campaigns depend on the premise that the more a person sacrifices for others, the more morally virtuous he is. In short, we have ample reason to use "altruism" as Rand did, signifying the belief that self-sacrifice is one's highest duty.[1]

The Relationship between Value and Virtue

Swanton believes that for Rand, since what counts as an objective value is determined in part by virtue concepts, what counts as being in one's interest and as a sacrifice are also determined in part by virtue. This is what distances Rand's egoism from the baser egoism that "common sense and decency," as Swanton puts it, would reject.

I don't think that this is Rand's view, however. I could see why one might think that a particular thing (such as a job) that may initially seem

---

1. Politicians in the United States routinely invoke our noble "duty to serve." In his 2004 presidential campaign, John Kerry was not inviting debate, but uttering a platitude that he could count on virtually everyone agreeing with, when he said: "And whatever our faith, one belief should bind us all: The measure of our character is our willingness to give of ourselves for others and for our country" (acceptance speech at the Democratic National Convention, 29 July 2004, http://www.washingtonpost.com/wp-dyn/articles/A25678-2004Jul29.html). Thanks to Greg Salmieri for calling this passage to my attention. It is also worth bearing in mind that many utilitarians, among others, notoriously advocate the sacrifice of self-interest for the good of the group.

to be a value for a person—objectively good for his flourishing—may not be, in fact, because its acquisition would require the violation of a virtue. But that means that it is not really good for him, that it is not in his interest. Virtues *are* virtues, in Rand's view, *on the grounds* that their exercise is necessary in order for the results of one's actions to be genuinely valuable. The role of virtues is not to introduce some other kind of consideration, besides the agent's interest, that carries a distinct "portion" of morality's authority. Rand would agree that a person should not benefit another if that constitutes a "nonvirtuous" sacrifice. But what *makes* certain traits virtuous is that they advance agents' objective interests. Thus I agree with the excerpt quoted from Kelley, if I understand it correctly: virtue depends on value.[2]

This is not to say that a rational egoist "makes up" what is virtuous as he goes along, depending on what he reckons valuable or in his interest on an ad hoc basis. Rather, the requirements of human survival dictate the broad practical principles that a person must adhere to in order to flourish. The major moral virtues name those principles. By exercising these virtues, a person is serving his interest; by spurning them, he is undermining it. What's crucial, though, is that virtues' claim on him stems entirely from those virtues' service to his well-being.[3] A rational egoist's practice of virtue reflects no inhibition of his pursuit of his interest.

This is worth emphasizing because, in a few places, Swanton's discussion suggests the belief that for Rand, virtue serves as a "check" that disciplines egoism. Swanton thinks that Rand views independence as a noninstrumental virtue, for example, since Rand describes it as reflecting the basic choice between surviving by the work of one's own mind or as a parasite fed by the minds of others (cf. Smith 2006, 113). But in fact, being a parasite isn't wrong *because* it is "ignoble." Rand meant "parasite" literally. Parasitism is not a viable means of survival for human beings (as it is for certain other organisms). The reason that Rand endorses acting by the

2. The passage from Kelley (2001, 69) reads: "Virtue is a derivative aspect of flourishing in the sense that what counts as a virtuous action, policy, or trait of character depends on prior assumptions about what things are valuable." The full explanation of the relationship between virtues and values is more involved, however.

3. It is true that, in a particular decision-making situation, a person's reminding himself of the virtues can sometimes help him to see the bigger picture and recognize what things would truly be values to him. He might appreciate, for instance, that what initially seems to be the self-interested course actually would not be. This is not because, at the foundational level of establishing which types of actions are virtuous, virtue precedes value, however. Rather, it is because something's being a virtue is itself grounded in its service to individuals' self-interest.

work of one's own mind is that the alternative (parasitism) doesn't work. Obviously, a person might get by to some extent for awhile by freeloading off first-handed others, but as a consistently practiced policy, parasitism will not get the job done; it is not, in principle, the path to human life. Human survival depends on reality-grounded thinking and acting (which is what independence calls for), rather than other-people-grounded "thinking" and acting (parasitism).

In short, it *is* ignoble to be a parasite *because* it works against your interest. Standards of "nobility" are of a piece with the standard of moral evaluation: human life (see Smith 2006, chap. 5).

This misreading surfaces again in Swanton's assessment that Rand agrees with Aristotle in holding that friendship, pleasure, etc. are values only when "excellent" or "proper." What's crucial for Rand, however, is that certain things are "excellent" or "proper" *because* they are life-enhancing. Swanton objects that what is "proper" is normative and controversial, implying (I *think*) that definitive answers could never be given. That relevant theories are controversial does not mean that they are all equally valid, however. Rand argues (and she is hardly alone in this) that the normative is grounded in the factual (see Wright 2005; Wright 2008; Smith 2000, chaps. 4–5). Just as conclusions about proper nutrition for kangaroos, proper activity for tigers, or ideal conditions for growing roses are rooted in facts about those things' natures, so what is good for human beings is so rooted. Given the aim of life, facts about living organisms set the "shoulds."

I'd readily agree that this is an area where more work needs to be done, fleshing out the character of ideal life for human beings in greater detail and tracing the links between values in such a life and the specific virtues. This work would be valuable for anyone interested in naturalistic ethics. But the immediate point is that "spiritual" values are not deemed values by some criterion other than their contribution to survival. Certain pleasures and spiritual goods are part of human life's requirements—which is why Rand regards these particular things (such as friendship, art, self-esteem) as values. They serve to enhance one's enjoyment of life and appetite for life, both of which are necessary to fuel a person's making the effort to act in life-advancing ways. The state of a person's *psyche* can make a significant difference to his survival. Rand's recognition of spiritual values reflects her respect for the complex psychological/physical organisms that human beings are. (On the importance of a person's psychological health, see Smith 2000, 136–45.)

Insufficient Concern for Others

Swanton's final concern is that Rand's view grants insufficient attention to others, as it has no basis for criticizing those who have an "excessively narrow" conception of others' interests in which *they* have a stake. Essentially, Rand's "altruism" isn't altruistic enough.

But that shouldn't be a surprise—because Rand does not endorse altruism, "virtuous" or any other kind. The only way for a human being to flourish, she argues, is by acting as his nature dictates is necessary, to achieve that—by acting egoistically, so as to attain his flourishing. This does not exclude engagement in all sorts of beneficial and enjoyable relationships with others, but those are to be pursued *when and because* they make a positive net contribution to the agent's welfare.

What is the case against Rand on this charge? The assurance that Kant and virtue ethicists "have resources" for defending a claim that a person "ought to be appropriately benevolent to others with whom he has no sympathy" is far from a demonstration of the propriety of altruism (whether moderate or extreme). In fact, it skirts the pivotal question of how much benevolence is "appropriate"—a self-sacrificial amount or not?—and it begs the question of why it is appropriate. What *makes* some benevolence "appropriate"? What makes certain conceptions of one's interest "excessively narrow" and others "suitably broad"? Indeed, why must egoism be compatible with "virtuous altruism"? Why is that the test? Swanton relies on major substantive assumptions that highlight the differences between altruism and egoism but which fail to provide justification for altruism.

Swanton does argue that "better" forms of egoism can "show that an inability to have a stake in relevant others' interests may constitute deficiency in affective states, and a lack of virtue." The unsympathetic moralist is flawed in his empathy. What this doesn't establish, as far as I can tell, though, is why this constitutes a *moral* deficiency. Swanton seems to be assuming that moral propriety requires empathy toward others. (In fact, whether a person's lack of empathy in a given case is a defect, morally or in any other respect, depends on whether the other person warrants it.)

This all gets rather tangled because emotions and affective dispositions are not the standard of morality, for Rand, and because "benevolence" isn't what is actually in dispute. Again, as I intimated earlier: Rand opposes self-sacrifice. She does not oppose benevolence. (On the implications of Rand's egoism for kindness, generosity, and charity, see Smith 2006, chap. 10.)

So, to address a final question raised by Swanton: would Rand "de-plore" empathy and the "emotional promptings of altruism?" Notice that this bundles distinct questions. Empathy is not necessarily a disposition to engage in self-sacrifice, as altruists do not enjoy a monopoly on empa-thy. Moreover, if empathy is understood as an emotion, Rand would not "deplore" it, or evaluate it *morally,* at all. If empathy is not an emotion, but a disposition to action, then Rand would evaluate it as healthy or not on the basis of the kind of action it inclines one to take: either the action is consonant with one's interest or antithetical to that interest.

Swanton is right that Rand doesn't offer a rationale for self-sacrificial assistance to others. She doesn't aspire to do so. If that's a deficiency in Rand's view, that needs to be *shown.*

What Is Included in Virtue?

LESTER H. HUNT

There is certainly a great deal in Tara Smith's wonderful book that is worth discussing and pondering. From the many possible topics I will select one, simply on the grounds that it touches on matters that I have thought about and written on myself. It is a point on which I seem to disagree with her.

Smith remarks, in her preliminary discussion of the nature of virtue in general, that Rand's conception of virtue differs from many traditional ones in two ways. First, many traditional theories hold that a virtue is a trait of character. In Rand's view it is not. Second, many traditional views hold that virtue involves doing the "the proper action with a certain spirit and inclination," whereas Rand denies that "a particular feeling on a given occasion is a requirement of moral virtue" (Smith 2006, 51). The latter denial is a potentially deep difference between Rand and the Aristotelian tradition. It has often been remarked that a basic difference between Aristotle and Kant is that Kant sees virtue, by nature, as standing in opposition to "inclination" (*Neigung*), while in Aristotle the closest concept he has to this "inclination" actually appears to be *part of what virtue is*. Aristotle actually distinguishes between virtue (*aretê*) and the strength of will that enables one to do the right thing despite inclinations to the contrary (*enkrateia*). For him, the need to struggle to do the right thing suggests that you aren't fully virtuous. This difference between Aristotle and Kant rests, I think, on a deeper difference, between their views on the relation (or lack of one) between emotion and reason. What I find puzzling is that both Smith and Rand are on Aristotle's side on this deeper issue. It seems to me that they ought to agree with him on the less fundamental issue, about the nature of virtue, as well. In addition, I have a suspicion—and I will put this forth with great trepidation—that Smith has misinterpreted Rand on this point, or rather that she has overinterpreted a peculiarity of the way Rand expresses herself in certain passages in her works.

The underlying difference between Kant and Aristotle, as I understand it, is this. Kant thinks of inclinations, and for the most part emotions in general, as irrational impulses, in the sense that they are not guided by the agent's mind. Though one's emotional constitution is capable of being shaped by one's moral education, the part of one's training that accomplishes this is the part that proceeds by rote and drill. It takes place independently of the child's still-undeveloped capacity to grasp practical principles. It is a sort of training to which not only human beings but also animals are subjected (Kant 1960, esp. chap. 2; see also Hunt 1997, 6–9). Kant defines "inclination" as "the dependence of the power of appetition on sensation" (*Groundwork*, Ak. 413n [1998]). What he appears to mean by this is that what goes on in this part of the agent's consciousness is due purely to what sensory experiences one has, and not to any thinking one has done on the conceptual level. Suppose we add to these ideas the plausible assumption that things that take place in the entirely subconceptual part of one's mind are automatic, unchosen. Then we immediately get an interesting ethical result, namely, that one gets no moral credit for such things. One might, however, get moral credit for the fact that one resists and overcomes such factors, just as one does for resisting and overcoming external obstacles. And that, of course, is Kant's view.

For present purposes, the notion in Aristotle's ethics that corresponds most closely to Kant's idea of "inclination" is "passion" (*pathos*). Aristotle speaks of the passions as *logoi enuloi* (*De Anima* I.1 403a25). However one decides to translate this curious expression—embodied ideas? en-mattered essences?—it obviously is meant to suggest that the passions represent a region of overlap between conceptions and sensations, or between the mind and the body. Aristotle, as far as we know, never developed his views on this subject, but one plausible way to begin to do so would be this. Though it is generally true that passions are automatic and unchosen, they are the automatic and unchosen consequences of one's evaluative thoughts and judgments. If I react with fear to an unexpected turn of events, it is because I judge it to be a threat to something I value, and this in turn is the result of a lifetime of experience and thinking (or failures to think) about which turns of events are and which are not threats, and which things I should and should not value. Most of this is material that I am not consciously aware of at the present moment, but its practical import is encapsulated in my present emotional reaction and in the resulting desire to neutralize the perceived threat somehow or other. (For a closely related view, see Arnold 1960, chap. 9.)

I would argue that this way of developing the relation between passions and thoughts changes everything, as far as the ethical import of emotional responses is concerned, opening up possibilities that differ sharply from the Kantian position. There are two reasons for this. First, my emotional reactions reveal much about what it is that I really value. Second, a great many of the inputs into the thinking and failing to think that resulted in my values are factors that are chosen by me. What my emotions reveal about me, to a significant extent at any rate, is *my values as formed and conditioned by my choices*. That is actually close to being a statement of what it is about me that can be ethically good or bad. For completeness, we may only need to add *as revealed in my actions*. If this is right, then the emotions that lie behind my actions can be ethically very significant.

This brings us back to the first of the two denials that I referred to at the outset: Smith's denial that virtue is a trait of character. If the ethical value of one's actions is to some extent based on the values from which they spring, then the acts of a virtuous person cannot exist in isolation. If my values really are my values, and consequently are embodied in my emotions, then I will characteristically act in the appropriate ways. And this does mean having traits of character.

As I have already suggested, the Aristotelian view of the emotions I have just imagined is just the one that Rand herself held. Indeed, Smith quite properly points this out in her book, though in a different chapter (and a different context) from the one I quoted earlier. As she tells us, an emotion for Rand is "an affective response to a subconscious evaluation of a perceived or considered object" (2006, 70). For this reason, "emotions are the voice of values in one's consciousness" (71). Obviously, we are dealing with something like Aristotelian *pathê* here, and not Kantian *Antrieben*.

I also suggest, though with the appropriate trepidation, that there is reason to think that Rand drew the Aristotelian conclusion that virtue, at least consummate virtue of the highest sort, includes as a part of itself not only the act but the spirit in which it is done. In a letter to John Hospers, she said: "Do you accept reason vs. emotions as a dichotomy? . . . In a man of fully rational, fully integrated convictions, emotions follow the judgments of reason as an unforced, automatic response" (*Letters* 526). This is just what would seem to follow from the Aristotelian view of the emotions. In a person whose real values are perfectly rational and consistent, there will be no basic conflict between the emotions, nor between emotions and reason. Moreover, she is clearly saying, and quite rightly in my opinion, that a life that is integrated in this way is higher, better than one that is not.

I think the most eloquent evidence on this exegetical point comes from a source that Smith does not use very much, namely, the characterizations of the heroes of Rand's novels. Smith inevitably relies on the things that these characters *say* as evidence for Rand's ethical views, but I think we are missing a rich source of material if we do not also look closely at what these characters *are*. Rand famously described her overriding purpose in writing her novels like this: "This is the motive and purpose of my writing: *the projection of an ideal man*. The portrayal of a moral ideal, as my ultimate literary goal, as an end in itself—to which any didactic, intellectual or philosophical values contained in a novel are only the means" (from "The Goal of My Writing," a speech given in 1963, printed in *RM* 162). In order to understand just what that ideal is, we should of course look at what Howard Roark says in *The Fountainhead*, but we should also look at how he acts, thinks, and feels. Here again I can to *some* extent quote Smith's words to support my case. She points out that "in her journals, Rand describes . . . Howard Roark . . . as acting, when confronting difficult decisions involving his values, as if he sees only one choice open to him." Smith draws, admittedly, a rather different conclusion from this evidence than I would. She says: "Rand sees no value in struggle per se" (2006, 52). That is, Roark would get no extra moral credit, as it were, if he had to wrestle with himself, Kant-style, in order to make the right choice. This is, of course, true. But surely there is more to it than that. Surely many of *The Fountainhead*'s millions of readers have sensed that the wonderful serenity with which Roark does things that most of us would do, if at all, only with a struggle against ourselves is part of what indicates how good (that is, how virtuous) he is.

This feature of his character is evinced in many scenes in the book, but one of the most eloquent, partly because it is one in which Roark is most severely tested, is the one in which he turns down the Manhattan Bank Company commission. It is a commission he desperately needs. If he does not get it, he will have to close his office, at least for the time being. At the beginning of the meeting, Mr. Weidler, the company's agent, says, "Well, Mr. Roark, the commission's yours." Roark simply bows his head: "It was best not to trust his voice for a few minutes." He soon learns, though, that there is a condition attached to this offer. He must change the building's too-radical appearance, incorporating Greek elements throughout its facade, "to give the public the *impression* of what they are accustomed to." The scene continues: "Roark got up. He had to stand. He concentrated on the effort of standing. It made the rest easier. He leaned on one straight arm, his hand closed over the edge of the table, the tendons showing under the skin of his wrist." He speaks at length, explaining why the requested changes would spoil the building's integrity, but to no avail. The decision has already been made: if he does not accept the compromise, the commission will go to someone else, someone more malleable. So Mr. Weidler can only put the question to him:

> "You understand the situation, Mr. Roark?"
>
> "Yes," said Roark. His eyes were lowered. He was looking down at the drawings.
>
> "Well?"
>
> Roark did not answer.
>
> "Yes or no, Mr. Roark?"
>
> Roark's head leaned back. He closed his eyes.
>
> "No," said Roark.
>
> After a while, the chairman asked:
>
> "Do you realize what you are doing?"
>
> "Quite," said Roark. (*Fountainhead* 194–96)

The reader knows that during those pauses in the conversation, Roark is not, or not primarily, struggling to defeat his urge to accept the commission and compromise. To some extent, he is merely, as it were, watching the collapse of the hopes raised by Mr. Weidler's offer moments before, given what Roark is sure he must do.

Rand's description of Roark's speech to the bank company officials obviously applies to much more than its explicit subject: "He explained why an honest building, like an honest man, had to be of one piece and one faith; what constituted the life source, the idea in any existing thing or creature, and why—if one smallest part committed treason to that idea—the thing or creature was dead; and why the good, the high, and the noble on earth was only that which kept its integrity" (*Fountainhead* 194–96). Rand is applying the same ideal, a certain conception of loyalty to one's underlying theme, to the aesthetic issues of architecture and to the ethical issues of human life. One of the things that she is expressing, as far as the ethical issues are concerned, is the particular virtue of integrity, which Smith explains so well in chapter 7 of her book. This virtue is a certain consistency between one's actions and one's explicit values. But the quoted passage could also be taken as referring to the same sort of consistency among one's values, and between one's thoughts about those values and one's emotions about them. Seen in the context of the characterization of Roark, which glowingly illustrates these sorts of consistency, it is actually hard to avoid taking the passage in this way.

The general issue of the importance, for virtue and vice, of the "spirit" in which one acts is eloquently expressed, though in a very different way, by Roark's antipode in *The Fountainhead*, Peter Keating. Here is a person whose outward behavior is often, at least in the earlier parts of the narrative, quite attractive and charming. With his boyish ebullience, it seems to the people around him that he values them for their virtues and that he is excited about his new job at the firm of Francon and Heyer because it is an opportunity to produce things that are good. The author shows us, by showing his actions *from the inside*, that none of this is true. His apparent friendliness has little to do with genuine benevolence. Except in relation to Roark and Catherine Halsey, he is simply a user. Other than in these two relationships, which until his character has disintegrated are his points of contact with decency and values, he is constantly striving to manipulate or defraud others to confer on him a false semblance of value, which consists mainly in being admired. In this way, virtually everything he does, although pleasant and likeable to the casual observer, is actually profoundly corrupt. I have long thought that Rand's characterization of Keating is one of the most vivid and convincing presentations of the idea that, as far as ethical value is concerned, the spirit in which one acts is very important.

Smith makes it fairly clear how she would answer at least some of the things I have said. Soon after her comment contrasting Rand's view of virtue with views in which virtue includes doing things with "a certain spirit and inclination," she says: "The more naturally inclined a person feels toward performing a particular proper action, the more likely he is to do it. If the action is indeed rationally egoistic, then he stands to benefit from that affective disposition" (2006, 51). Of course, this sounds initially like an argument on my side of this issue. If your conception of virtue is egoistic, and feeling naturally inclined to do the right thing is a character-state that is in the agent's interest, then why isn't it (perhaps with relevant qualifications) a part of what virtue is? The answer, Smith says, has to do with agent control: "Nonetheless, Rand rejects the idea that a particular feeling on a given occasion is a requirement of moral virtue for the simple reason that feelings are not under a person's direct control. . . . We might take actions that can eventually alter some of our inclinations, such as engaging in psychological therapy, but we cannot directly and immediately manipulate our emotions and inclinations, as they are largely a product of subconscious premises. And morality cannot fairly demand what a person is incapable of delivering" (51–52). Up to a point, what she is saying here is very plausible. What morality demands or requires must be in one's direct control. But I am also fairly sure of the proposition that some things that are ethically good or bad are not things that are directly in our control. I suppose I should conclude from this that the content of virtue and vice, the difference between the ethically good and the ethically bad, is not exhausted by what morality demands us to do or not do.

Before I comment further on this conclusion, I obviously should say more about this proposition of which I say that I am fairly sure. Here is an example. When Roark is designing a building, he is doing something that is admirable. When Keating is designing a building, he is doing something that is—well, the opposite of admirable. As I have suggested, part of the difference between them is the purpose with which each of them acts. Roark does it in order to achieve the rich complex of values that a great building can embody. Keating does it to stun his clients, impress the critics, and win the admiration of people whose opinion he has no reason to respect. Is this feature of the situation in the direct control of both of them? I think the answer is no. For one thing, the word "purpose" here constitutes a rather crude simplification. One thing that is virtuous about the way Roark does what he does is his total dedication to the values involved, the sharp difference between the importance these things have for him and the importance he places on other, lesser goods. Is Keating ever capable of *that*? Probably not.

Further, whether one is pursuing a given ethically relevant purpose at all may not always be in one's direct control. There is a very sad sequence of scenes involving Peter Keating near the end of the novel that I think illustrates this point very well. He has lost his popularity with clients and critics and, without the one prop on which he had always leaned, every aspect of his life and character begins to disintegrate rapidly. He will soon make an open confession of mediocrity to Roark and beg him, as his own last chance to save his career, to design the Cortland housing project for him. In the midst of all of this, for no obvious reason, he remembers his childhood ambition (abandoned because his mother thought architecture was more "respectable") of becoming a painter. He rents a shack in the hills and furtively, unknown to anyone else, tries to paint: "He had a quiet pain as sole conception of what he wanted to express, a humble, unbearable tenderness for the sight of the earth around him—and something tight, paralyzed as sole means to express it. He went on. He tried. . . . There was no pleasure in it, no pride, no solution; only—while he sat alone before the easel—a sense of peace" (*Fountainhead* 590). What is it that he is trying to do here, and yet is unable to do? I don't think it is a matter merely of lost artistic abilities. It isn't that he has the same goals that a real artist has, but has allowed his technical abilities to get rusty. He has lost more than that. To some extent, he wishes to want goals that the artist seeks, but no longer knows how.

Clearly, though, the reader is meant to realize that Keating is the way he is now because of past choices. Once, in the past, he had a chance to avoid becoming what he is now, but it is too late. Further, the actions he could have taken in the past to avoid becoming what he is now were the indirect, imperfect sorts of measures that Smith mentions in the passage I quoted earlier: engaging in psychological therapy and the like. Yet surely this indirect and perhaps imperfect degree of control is enough to allow us to blame him for the way he presently is.

My own view is that the move from an ethics of duties to do particular actions to an ethics of virtue probably requires us to loosen somewhat the condition that credit and blame presuppose that the agent you are admiring or blaming had a strong, direct sort of control over the things for which you give him credit or blame. In my view, the idea behind an ethics of virtue is that ethical value resides not merely in what particular things you do but also in what sort of person you are. It probably is true that I have less control, or less direct control, over the sort of person I am than over which particular acts I do.

Perhaps we should say that what morality "demands" or "requires," to use Smith's words once more, does presuppose a strong, direct sort of control. But perhaps not all ethical principles are demands or requirements. What else could they be? Well, I would say that they could be *ideals*. That, after all, is a word Rand often used to describe the heroes of her fiction (see *RM* 162). One of the most effective ways to state a moral ideal is to describe a character-type. This is what I have always thought Rand was doing.

If Tara Smith's interpretation of Rand's ethics is right, if "virtue" for Rand is not a trait of character, does not include a propensity to act in characteristic ways, does not include acting with the proper spirit or inclination, and does not include emotions as part of itself, then in what sense is Rand's ethics a virtue ethics at all? Rand expressed her views by using the word "virtue" frequently, but of course one could also set forth a Kantian or utilitarian view using that word. Is she really practicing virtue ethics, in the sense in which Aristotle and Nietzsche were, or is her virtue ethics, on Smith's interpretation, merely a matter of word choice?

The Primacy of Action in Virtue
Response to Hunt

TARA SMITH

Lester Hunt is concerned that by my account, Rand does not consider virtue to be a trait of character or to be something that requires proper action to be taken with the right "spirit and inclination." Indeed, Hunt wonders whether such a Rand is truly a virtue ethicist. I stand by my portrait of Rand, but I actually think that some of our differences are relatively minor; I agree with much in the spirit of what Hunt is saying. I also welcome his use of further examples from and references to Rand's fiction. I didn't make more use of those in the book because I couldn't assume that my audience would be familiar with it and I feared that the explanations needed to make clear the import of various events would be far too lengthy. But Rand's fiction *is* a helpful resource in exploring her view. I would caution, though, that Rand's standards and intent in fiction were self-consciously different from what they were in philosophy proper. She did not write fiction simply as a means of clarifying her philosophy or conveying her moral theory, she said many times (see *Letters* 157–58; *RM* 162–64, 169–70; and *AON* 153–54; see also *Letters* 631–32, for a statement on how to interpret the philosophical ideas presented in fiction).

Is Rand a Virtue Ethicist?

I am not particularly invested in classifying Rand as a virtue ethicist. In fact, I don't classify her as such in my book. As far as I can tell, nothing important hinges on her being one. I don't mean to be glib about this. I do, in the book's introduction, refer to recent attention to the virtues and to naturalism and commend attention to Rand against that background. But my book focuses on the meat of her theory, the substance of the virtues that explain how to lead a rationally selfish life, rather than on the style or form of the guidance (Smith 2006, 4; see also my explanation of how Rand's view straddles the conventional virtue-principle divide, 50–52). Indeed, *this* is what's striking and radical in her theory, not her stance in recent debates over virtue ethics. Whether Rand's view qualifies as a virtue ethics will obviously depend on the criteria, moreover, a subject that is itself disputed among virtue ethicists. She definitely rejects the "primacy of virtue" belief that virtues dictate values. But my main point is that I don't think it matters much whether she is one. My concern is to figure out what Rand's view is and, ultimately, how valid her view is. I'd need to be convinced that virtue ethics is the only viable ethics before treating that as an essential desideratum in evaluating her theory.

Rand Is More Aristotelian than Smith Portrays

The central question in Hunt's chapter is whether I've got Rand's view right, so let's turn to that. Hunt contends that Rand is more Aristotelian than I make out. He includes the manner with which a person does the right thing, the spirit and feeling of an action, and reasons that "my emotional reactions reveal much about what it is that I really value." Moreover, he says, "a great many of the inputs into the thinking and failing to think that resulted in my values are factors that are *chosen by me.* What my emotions reveal about me, to a significant extent, at any rate, is *my values as formed and conditioned by my choices*" (first emphasis added).

I agree with both statements, on the understanding that what "I really value" is not the same as what I have consciously contemplated and deliberately chosen to value. Emotions *are* the "voice of values," as Hunt quotes me saying, but not only of our consciously affirmed values. (They are also the voice of beliefs, in Rand's view, and what I am about to say applies to both beliefs and values; see Smith 2006, 70–73.) Some values may be held subconsciously. A person's values are not all necessarily thought out or the results of dedicated deliberation. For example, maybe I value pleasing my father because I adopted that value at a very young age, subconsciously, without good reason. I may be well into adulthood before realizing that I retain the attitude that "pleasing father is an especially important imperative." This might be a value I would now reject, but it may well have exerted considerable influence over my dispositions over the years (to feel hurt by his disapproval, for instance, or to seek to avoid that disapproval). Even my recognition today that pleasing him isn't *so* important may not immediately dissolve all the inclinations that have grown out of that premise, over the years. (This is why therapy can take a long time to be effective.) Similarly, a faulty generalization reached from childhood experience of an erratic parent—"you can't trust other people; it's safer not to get close, people will burn you"—may naturally affect my disposition to be emotionally intimate with others.

My point is simply that we do not completely control our emotions. More exactly, I should say: we do not *directly* and currently, immediately, control our emotions. I agreed with Hunt's statements because I take seriously his qualifications: "to a significant extent," my values are formed by my choices; "a great many" of the inputs to my values are chosen. But not all of them are knowingly and deliberately chosen. And this is what's important to a person's moral responsibility. I agree that through our actions, over an extended period, we make ourselves certain kinds of people, with particular kinds of emotional "sets" or dispositions. In this way, a person does bear responsibility for some of his feelings and inclinations. But it is not the case that a person chooses all his beliefs and values as a mature, fully informed and rationally capable adult, such that any "wayward" emotions he experiences are proof of moral failings. It would be unjust to fault a person for something he is currently incapable of (for feeling differently), as he may be if he hasn't had reason to suspect the destructive "baggage" from childhood that is impeding his responding in the most healthy ways. Just as there are aspects of our physical health that we do not control, there are aspects of our psychological health that we do not control.

The Ideal Man

Hunt observes that my view treats moral principles as demands or requirements. Yet not all of them are, he objects; some are ideals. Rand wrote (in a passage clearly referring to her fiction writing) that the motive and purpose of her writing was "*the projection of an ideal man*" (*RM* 162). And she refers, in that passage, to the portrayal of a moral ideal. Nonetheless, the problem I see is that "an ideal man" encompasses more than a morally ideal man. Rand's purpose in fiction transcended her purpose when prescribing moral philosophy.

Consider Roark's "serenity" in seeing only one road open to him when facing choices that others would find difficult. Hunt says that part of what this conveys is how good, how virtuous Roark is. Something in this claim seems right. (Indeed, this is where I am most attracted to Hunt's view.) Yet is Roark more moral, in that action, than the man who has to struggle before doing what he should? The lack of struggle suggests that Roark has a more developed, more settled moral character, but that doesn't necessarily point to the moral inferiority of the other man's action. That man's struggle might result from the sorts of lingering subconscious premises that I referred to above.

A simple distinction might explain some of Hunt's and my differences here. The morality of a person's character and the morality of his action on a particular occasion are not necessarily the same. My character could be morally superior to my action on a given occasion (when through an uncharacteristic lapse, my action is not up to my usual high moral standards), just as my action could be morally superior to my character (as when I am in the process of improving my heretofore middling moral character). Thus Aristotle may be right that your need to struggle to do the right thing suggests that *you* aren't fully virtuous. When assessing a person, virtue implies that one does the right thing characteristically and relatively easily, as Roark does and as Hunt emphasizes. But when assessing an action, such a style of action may not be required. The conditions of being a virtuous person and the conditions of being a virtuous action are not identical.[1]

Beyond this distinction, though, my larger point is that Roark is an aesthetic ideal, as well as a moral one. Not everything that makes him the former—including his lack of internal conflict—is vital to his being the latter. To see this, think about some of Rand's other characters. Dominique, in *The Fountainhead*, is quite conflicted. Is this a moral failing? And is Roark, in loving her, compromising his moral standards?

1. The full and exact relationship between the two is more complex than this brief treatment might suggest, and I don't wish to exaggerate the separation between the two. Hunt's counsel that this relationship warrants further investigation is quite right, I think.

No. Dominique's is a deficit of understanding. Rand was emphatic that breaches of morality must be distinguished from errors of knowledge (*Atlas* 1059; see also Peikoff 1991, 223; and *Journals* 556, 626). Rand once described Dominique's particular error as "one from which many good people suffer" (albeit, in a less extreme form): "*the malevolent universe premise*: the belief that the good has no chance on earth, that it is doomed to lose" (*Q&A* 191).[2] Notice that the mistake is a mistaken belief. Good people make it. It is not a defect of moral character.

In *Atlas Shrugged*, Hank Rearden is another conflicted figure, yet morally, he is clearly a hero. Over the course of the novel, it is not a growth in his moral stature that enables him to eliminate those conflicts, but his growing understanding of the nature of his enemies and of some of his own mistaken premises. Eddie Willers is not one of the heroes of *Atlas*—not on a par with Galt, Rearden, Francisco, or Dagny—yet morally, he's a saint.

It is no accident that Rand's heroes are figures of well-above-average intelligence. They are not only morally admirable; they are ideal in many respects: smart, good-looking, physically healthy and fit. Yet in her non-fiction, Rand does not say that the moral man must exercise all of the virtues *and* must have a high IQ, attractive appearance, and so on. When she defines moral perfection as "unbreached rationality," she does not add: "*and:* no unhealthy emotional baggage from your upbringing, good genes, high-powered creative abilities, not being confined to a wheelchair, etc." (See Smith 2006, chap. 9, on the virtue of pride.)

So again, my basic thought is that it is a mistake to equate the ideal man portrayed in Rand's fiction with her moral ideal.[3]

---

2. I recommend reading the entirety of Rand's answer on this question, as well as my account of Dominique in Smith 2007, especially 298–301.

3. And this is why, while I agree with Hunt that Rand's letter to John Hospers (*Letters* 526) indicates her belief that an integrated life devoid of internal emotional conflict is "better" than the alternative, it does not indicate that she regards such a life as necessarily morally better in the sense of indicating a superior moral character.

Although it concerns a somewhat different issue, I should also register that I disagree with Hunt's interpretation of Keating as an illustration of the idea that the spirit in which one acts is important to ethical value. That Keating's actions may be "likeable to the casual observer" does not show that they are proper actions. What Keating is *after* is all wrong, not merely the manner in which he pursues it. The main problem with Keating, as I understand it, is not his insincerity, nor is it his pain and strain in doing the right thing. Rather, it is his lack of genuine ego. Consider, as evidence, Rand's journal entry describing him as "an empty space," the scene in which Dagny exposes this, and Keating's own realization of his self-betrayal in an encounter with Catherine (all are noted in Smith 2006, 109, 121).

Why Action Is Primary in Virtue

Finally, then, the most basic reason that I think that action (rather than spirit or inclination) is primary, in Rand's account of virtue, is her conception of the nature and function of ethics: "a code of values to guide man's choices and actions—the choices and actions that determine the purpose and the course of his life" (*VOS* 13; see also Smith 2006, 48–52). Ethics is emphatically not an aesthetic issue, in Rand's view. She emphasizes our need for it—our critical and fundamental need, as our survival depends on taking the right kinds of actions. A human being must *do* certain things—*create* material values, *judge* others objectively, and so on, as the virtues describe—if he is to flourish. Character can be good insofar as it flows from and typically leads to actions of the life-advancing sort.

It *is* better to be "of a piece," with the comparatively effortless integrity of Roark, because such a person has made taking proper actions more natural and easy for himself. But it is better *because* such a person has made a lot of right choices in the past and is likely to continue to make such choices and take correlative actions in the future. The value of a person's character, however, is derivative from the value of his actions. Rational action is the fundamental requirement of human life, thus rational action is, fundamentally, what moral virtue requires.

UNIFORM ABBREVIATIONS OF WORKS BY AYN RAND

(with indication of the editions cited from)

Rand's philosophical output took many different forms (e.g., monographs, essay collections, journal entries, lecture courses subsequently transcribed—not to mention the novels, which contain specific philosophical content and are themselves philosophical novels), and some items appear in several different editions with differing pagination. Because there is not yet a standard edition of her works, we decided to adopt for the series this list of uniform abbreviations and a standard set of (easily accessible) editions to which to refer for page numbers in citations. (Note: Some early printings of the Centennial editions used a different pagination from the current ones on which we draw.)

*Centennial trade editions (with facsimile original covers), New York: Plume, 2005
**Centennial mass-market editions, New York: Signet, 2005

Anthem   *Anthem* (*1953)

Anthem '38   *Anthem* (London: Cassells, 1938)

AOF   *The Art of Fiction: A Guide for Writers and Readers*, ed. T. Boeckmann (New York: Plume, 2000)

AON   *The Art of Nonfiction: A Guide for Writers and Readers*, ed. R. Mayhew (New York: Plume, 2001)

ARL   *The Ayn Rand Letter, 1971–1976* (New Milford, CT: Second Renaissance Books, 1990)

Atlas   *Atlas Shrugged* (*1957)

Column   *The Ayn Rand Column: Written for the* Los Angeles Times, *with additional essays*, 2nd ed. (New Milford, CT: Second Renaissance Books, 1990)

CUI   *Capitalism: The Unknown Ideal* (**1966)

EAR *The Early Ayn Rand: A Selection from Her Unpublished Fiction*, ed. L. Peikoff (**1984)

Fountainhead *The Fountainhead* (*1943); "Introduction" Introduction to the twenty-fifth anniversary edition of *The Fountainhead* (New York: Bobbs-Merrill Co., 1968)

FTNI *For the New Intellectual: The Philosophy of Ayn Rand* (**1961)

ITOE *Introduction to Objectivist Epistemology*, expanded 2nd ed. (New York: Meridian, 1990)

Journals *Journals of Ayn Rand*, ed. D. Harriman (New York: Dutton, 1997)

Letters *Letters of Ayn Rand*, ed. M. S. Berliner (New York: Dutton, 1995)

Lexicon *The Ayn Rand Lexicon: Objectivism from A to Z*, ed. H. Binswanger, The Ayn Rand Library, vol. IV (New York: Plume, 1986)

Marginalia *Ayn Rand's Marginalia: Her Critical Comments on the Writings of Over Twenty Authors*, ed. R. Mayhew (New Milford, CT: Second Renaissance Books, 1995)

OS *Objectively Speaking: Ayn Rand Interviewed*, ed. M. Podritske and P. Schwartz (Lanham, MD: Lexington Books, 2009)

Plays *Three Plays: Night of January 16th; Ideal; Think Twice* (**2005)

PWNI *Philosophy: Who Needs It* (**1982)

Q&A *Ayn Rand Answers: The Best of Her Q & A*, ed. R. Mayhew (London: New American Library, 2005)

RM *The Romantic Manifesto: A Philosophy of Literature* (**1969)

ROTP *Return of the Primitive: The Anti-Industrial Revolution*, ed. P. Schwartz (New York: Plume, 1999)

TO *The Objectivist 1966–71* (New Milford, CT: Second Renaissance Books, 1990)

TON *The Objectivist Newsletter 1962–65* (New Milford, CT: Second Renaissance Books, 1990)

VOR *The Voice of Reason: Essays in Objectivist Thought*, ed. Leonard Peikoff, The Ayn Rand Library, vol. 5 (New York: Plume, 1990)

VOS *The Virtue of Selfishness: A New Concept of Egoism* (**1964)

WTL *We the Living* (New York: Random House, 1959)

WTL '36 *We the Living* (New York: Macmillan, 1936)

REFERENCES

Alston, William. 1985. Concepts of epistemic justification. *Monist* 68 (1): 57–89.

Annas, Julia. 1981. *Introduction to Plato's Republic.* Oxford: Clarendon Press.

———. 1993. *Morality of happiness.* New York: Oxford University Press.

———. 2005. Virtue ethics: What kind of naturalism? In *Virtue ethics, old and new,* ed. Stephen M. Gardiner, 11–29. Ithaca: Cornell University Press.

———. 2008. Virtue ethics and the charge of egoism. In Bloomfield 2008, 205–24.

Anscombe, G. E. M. 1958. Modern moral philosophy. *Philosophy* 33:1–19.

Arnold, Magda. 1960. *Emotion and personality.* Vol. 1. New York: Columbia University Press.

Badhwar, Neera. 1993. Altruism versus self-interest: Sometimes a false dichotomy. *Social Philosophy and Policy* 10:90–117.

———. 2001. Is virtue only a means to happiness? In *Is virtue only a means to happiness? An analysis of virtue and happiness in Ayn Rand's writings,* by Neera Badhwar, with commentaries by Jay Freidenberg, Lester Hunt, and David Kelley, 5–36. Objectivist Studies 4. Washington DC: The Objectivist Center.

Baier, Kurt. 1970. Why should we be moral? In *Readings in contemporary ethical theory,* ed. K. Pahel and M. Schiller, 427–41. Englewood Cliffs, NJ: Prentice Hall.

Batson, C. D. 1991. *The altruism question: Toward a social-psychological answer.* Hillsdale, NJ: Lawrence Erlbaum Associates.

Batson, C. D., B. D. Duncan, P. Ackerman, T. Buckley, and K. Birch. 1981. Is empathic emotion a source of altruistic motivation? *Journal of Personality and Social Psychology* 40:290–302.

Bernstein, Andrew. 2007. Understanding the "rape" scene in *The Fountainhead.* In Mayhew 2007, 201–8.

Binswanger, Harry. 1990. *The biological basis of teleological concepts*. Marina Del Rey, CA: Ayn Rand Institute Press.

———. 1992. Life-based teleology and the foundations of ethics. *Monist* 75 (1): 84–104.

Blackburn, Simon. 1998. *Ruling passions*. Oxford: Clarendon Press.

Bloomfield, Paul. 2000. Virtue epistemology and the epistemology of virtue. *Philosophy and Phenomenological Research* 50 (1): 23–43.

———. 2001. *Moral reality*. New York: Oxford University Press.

———, ed. 2008. *Morality and self-interest*. New York: Oxford University Press.

———. 2009. Archimedeanism and why metaethics matters. Vol. 4 of *Oxford Studies in Metaethics*, ed. R. Shafer-Landau. New York: Oxford University Press.

Branden, Nathaniel. 1962. *Who is Ayn Rand? An analysis of the novels of Ayn Rand, with a biographical essay by Barbara Branden*. New York: Random House.

Brink, David. 1989. *Moral realism and the foundations of ethics*. New York: Cambridge University Press.

Charles, David. 1995. Aristotle and modern realism. In Heinaman 1995, 135–72.

Cooper, John M. 1975. *Reason and human good in Aristotle*. Cambridge, MA: Harvard University Press.

Copp, David. 2001. Realist-expressivism: A neglected option for moral realism. *Social Philosophy and Public Policy* 18:1–13.

Cullyer, Helen. 2006. Ayn Rand's normative ethics: The virtuous egoist. *Notre Dame Philosophical Reviews*, November 2006, http://ndpr.nd.edu/review.cfm?id=8123.

Daniels, Norman. 1976. Wide reflective equilibrium and theory acceptance in ethics. *Journal of Philosophy* 76 (5): 256–82.

Darwall, Stephen, Allan Gibbard, and Peter Railton. 1997. Toward *fin de siècle* ethics: Some trends. In *Moral discourse and practice: Some philosophical approaches*, 3–47. New York: Oxford University Press.

Davis, Mark H. 1996. *Empathy: A social psychological approach*. Madison, WI: Westview Press.

Dawkins, Richard. 1976. *The selfish gene*. New York: Oxford University Press.

Den Uyl, Douglas, and Douglas Rasmussen. 1981. Nozick on the Randian argument. In *Reading Nozick: Essays on anarchy, state, and utopia*, ed. Jeffrey Paul, 232–69. Totowa, NJ: Rowman and Littlefield.

———. 1986. Life, teleology, and eudaimonia in the ethics of Ayn Rand. In *The philosophic thought of Ayn Rand*, ed. Douglas Den Uyl and Douglas Rasmussen, 63–80. Chicago: University of Illinois Press.

Donagan, Alan. 1977. *The theory of morality*. Chicago: University of Chicago Press.

Dworkin, Ronald. 1996. Objectivity and truth: You'd better believe it. *Philosophy and Public Affairs* 25 (2): 87–139.

Everson, Stephen. 1995. Aristotle and the explanation of evaluation: A reply to David Charles. In Heinaman 1995, 173–99.

Falk, W. D. 1963. Morality, self, and others. In *Morality and the language of conduct*, ed. H. N. Castaneda and G. Nakhnikian. Detroit: Wayne State University Press. Reprinted in Bloomfield 2008, 225–50.

———. 1986. *Ought, reasons, and morality: The collected papers of W. D. Falk.* Ithaca: Cornell University Press.

Foot, Philippa. 2001. *Natural goodness.* New York: Oxford University Press.

Frankena, William. 1966. The concept of morality. *Journal of Philosophy* 63:688–96.

Frankfurt, Harry. 2004. *Reasons of love.* Princeton, NJ: Princeton University Press.

Garner, Richard. 1990. On the genuine queerness of moral facts and properties. *Australasian Journal of Philosophy* 68:137–46.

Gewirth, Alan. 1978. *Reason and morality.* Chicago: University of Chicago Press.

———. 1984. Replies to my critics. In *Gewirth's ethical rationalism: Critical essays*, ed. Edward Regis Jr., 192–255. Chicago: University of Chicago Press.

Ghate, Onkhar. 2007. The basic motivation of the creators and the masses in *The Fountainhead.* In Mayhew 2007, 243–83.

Gibbard, Allan. 1994. *Wise choices, apt feelings.* Cambridge, MA: Harvard Univeristy Press.

Gotthelf, Allan. 2000. *On Ayn Rand.* Belmont, CA: Wadsworth Publishing.

———. 2011. The morality of life. In Gotthelf and Salmieri 2011.

Gotthelf, Allan, and Gregory Salmieri, eds. 2011. *Ayn Rand: A companion to her works and thought.* Oxford: Wiley-Blackwell.

Haack, Susan. 1995. *Evidence and inquiry.* Malden, MA: Blackwell Publishers.

Heinaman, Robert, ed. 1995. *Aristotle and moral realism.* Boulder, CO: Westview Press.

Hoffman, M. L. 1978. Psychological and biological perspectives on altruism. *International Journal of Behavioral Development* 1:323–39.

Horgan, Terry, and Mark Timmons. 2006. Cognitive expressivism. In *Metaethics after Moore*, ed. T. Horgan and M. Timmons, 255–98. New York: Oxford University Press.

Hunt, Lester H. 1997. *Character and culture.* Lanham, MD: Rowman and Littlefield.

Hurka, Thomas. 2001. *Virtue, vice, and value.* Oxford: Clarendon Press.

Hursthouse, Rosalind. 1999. *On virtue ethics.* New York: Oxford University Press.

Irwin, Terence. 2008. Scotus and the possibility of moral motivation. In Bloomfield 2008, 159–76.

Joyce, Richard. 2001. *The myth of morality*. New York: Cambridge University Press.

Kagan, Shelly. 1992. The structure of normative theory. In *Philosophical perspectives 6: Ethics 1992*, ed. James Tomberlin. Atascadero, CA: Ridgeview Publishing.

Kant, Immanuel. 1960. *Education*. Ann Arbor: University of Michigan Press.

———. 1996. *The metaphysics of morals*. Trans. Mary Gregor. New York: Cambridge University Press.

———. 1998. *Groundwork of the metaphysics of morals*. Ed. Mary Gregor. New York: Cambridge University Press.

Kelley, David. 1986. *The evidence of the senses: A realist theory of perception*. Baton Rouge: Louisiana State University Press.

———. 1991. Evidence and justification. *Reason Papers* 16:165–79.

———. 1992. Peikoff's summa. *IOS Journal* 1 (3), also at http://www.objectivist center.org/cth--37-Peikoffs_Summa.aspx.

———. 2001. Why virtue is a means to our ultimate end. In *Is virtue only a means to happiness? An analysis of virtue and happiness in Ayn Rand's writings*, by Neera Badhwar, with commentaries by Jay Freidenberg, Lester Hunt, and David Kelley, 61–71. Objectivist Studies 4. Washington DC: The Objectivist Center.

Khawaja, Irfan. 2003. Tara Smith's *Viable values: Life as the root and reward of morality*: A discussion. *Reason Papers* 26 (2003): 63–88.

———. 2008. *Foundationalism and the foundations of ethics*. PhD diss., University of Notre Dame.

Korsgaard, Christine. 1996a. From duty and for the sake of the noble: Kant and Aristotle on morally good action. In *Aristotle, Kant, and the Stoics: Rethinking happiness and duty*, ed. Stephen Engstrom and Jennifer Whiting, 203–36. New York: Cambridge University Press.

———. 1996b. *The sources of normativity*. New York: Cambridge University Press.

LeMorvan, Pierre. 2004. Arguments against direct realism and how to counter them. *American Philosophical Quarterly* 41 (3): 221–34.

Long, Roderick. 2000. *Reason and value: Aristotle versus Rand*. Washington DC: The Objectivist Center.

Machan, Tibor. 1982. Epistemology and moral knowledge. *Review of Metaphysics* 36 (1): 23–49.

MacIntyre, Alasdair. 1990. *First principles, final ends, and contemporary philosophical issues*. The Aquinas Lecture 1990. Milwaukee: Marquette University Press.

———. 2006. Moral relativism, truth, and justification. In *The tasks of philosophy*. Vol. 1, *Selected essays*, 52–73. New York: Cambridge University Press.

Mackie, John. 1977. *Ethics: Inventing right and wrong*. New York: Penguin Books.

Mauss, Marcel. 1954. *An essay on the gift: The reason and form of exchange in archaic societies*. Trans. Ian Cunnison. New York: Penguin Books.

May, Simon. 1999. *Nietzsche's ethics and his war on morality*. Oxford: Clarendon Press.

Mayhew, Robert, ed. 2007. *Essays on Ayn Rand's* The Fountainhead. Lanham, MD: Lexington Books, 2007.

McDowell, John. 1980. The role of eudaimonia in Aristotle's ethics. In *Essays on Aristotle's ehics*, ed. Amelie Oksenberg Rorty, 359–76. Berkeley: University of California Press.

———. 1988. Values and secondary qualities. In *Essays on moral realism*, ed. G. Sayre-McCord, 166–80. Ithaca: Cornell University Press.

———. 1995. Eudaimonism and realism in Aristotle's ethics. In Heinaman 1995, 201–18.

Moore, G. E. 1993. *Principia ethica*, rev. ed. Ed. Thomas Baldwin. New York: Cambridge University Press.

Nagel, Thomas. 1978. *The possibility of altruism*. Princeton, NJ: Princeton University Press.

Nietzsche, Friedrich. 1973. *Beyond good and evil*. Trans. R. J. Hollingdale. New York: Penguin Books.

———. 1974. *The gay science*. Trans. Walter Kaufmann. New York: Vintage Books.

———. 1976a. *Thus spoke Zarathustra*. In *The portable Nietzsche,* ed. and trans. Walter Kaufmann, 103–439. New York: Penguin Books.

———. 1976b. *Twilight of the idols*. In *The portable Nietzsche,* ed. and trans. Walter Kaufmann, 463–564. New York: Penguin Books.

———. 1984. *Human all too human*. Trans. Marion Faber with Stephen Lehmann. Lincoln: University of Nebraska Press.

———. 1996. *On the genealogy of morals*. Trans. Douglas Smith. New York: Oxford University Press.

———. 1997. *Untimely meditations*. Ed. Daniel Breazeale. Cambridge Texts in the History of Philosophy. New York: Cambridge University Press.

Nozick, Robert. 1974. *Anarchy, state, and utopia*. New York: Basic Books.

———. 1997. On the Randian argument. In *Socratic puzzles*. Cambridge, MA: Harvard University Press.

Peikoff, Leonard. 1991. *Objectivism: The philosophy of Ayn Rand*. New York: Dutton.

Plantinga, Alvin. 1993. *Warrant: The current debate*. New York: Oxford University Press.

Prichard, H. A. 1912. Does moral philosophy rest on a mistake? *Mind* 21:21–37.

Railton, Peter. 1986. Moral realism. *Philosophical Review* 95:163–207.

Rasmussen, Douglas B. 2002. Rand on obligation and value. *Journal of Ayn Rand Studies* 4 (1): 69–86.

———. 2005. Rand on obligation and value. In *Philosophers of capitalism: Menger, Mises, Rand, and beyond*, ed. Edward W. Younkins, 173–85. Lanham, MD: Lexington Books.

———. 2006. Regarding choice and the foundations of morality: Reflections on Rand's *Ethics. Journal of Ayn Rand Studies* 7 (2): 309–28.

———. 2007a. The Aristotelian significance of the section titles of *Atlas Shrugged*: A brief consideration of Rand's view of logic and reality. In *Ayn Rand's Atlas Shrugged: A philosophical and literary companion*, ed. Edward M. Younkins, 33–45. Aldershot: Ashgate Publishing.

———. 2007b. Rand's metaethics: Rejoinder to Hartford. *Journal of Ayn Rand Studies* 8 (2): 307–16.

Rawls, John. 1999a. Outline of a decision procedure for ethics. In *Collected papers*, ed. Samuel Freeman, 1–19. Cambridge, MA: Harvard University Press.

———. 1999b. *A theory of justice,* rev. ed. Cambridge, MA: Belknap Press of Harvard University Press.

Rorty, Richard. 1982. *Consequences of pragmatism*. Minneapolis: University of Minnesota Press.

Salmieri, Gregory. 2011. Values and the act of valuing. In Gotthelf and Salmieri 2011.

Scanlon, T. M. 1998. *What we owe to each other*. Cambridge, MA: Harvard University Press.

Schneewind, J. B. 1983. Moral knowledge and moral principles. In *Revisions: Changing perspectives in moral philosophy*, ed. Stanley Hauerwas and Alasdair MacIntyre, 113–26. South Bend: University of Notre Dame Press.

Shafer-Landau, Russ. 2003. *Moral realism: A defence*. New York: Oxford University Press.

Singer, Peter. 1993. *Practical ethics*, 2nd ed. New York: Cambridge University Press.

Smart, J. J. C. and Bernard Williams. 1973. *Utilitarianism: For and against*. New York: Cambridge University Press.

Smith, Michael. 1994. *The moral problem*. Malden, MA: Blackwell Publishing.

Smith, Tara. 1995. *Moral rights and political freedom*. Lanham, MD: Rowman and Littlefield.

———. 2000. *Viable values—A study of life as the root and reward of morality*. Lanham, MD: Rowman and Littlefield.

———. 2005. Egoistic friendship. *American Philosophical Quarterly* 42:263–77.

———. 2006. *Ayn Rand's normative ethics: The virtuous egoist*. New York: Cambridge University Press.

———. 2007. Unborrowed vision: Independence and egoism in *The Fountainhead*. In Mayhew 2007, 285–304.

Swanton, Christine. 2003. *Virtue ethics: A pluralistic view*. New York: Oxford University Press.

Timmons, Mark. 1999. *Morality without foundations: A defense of ethical contextualism*. New York: Oxford University Press.

Tresan, Jon. 2009. Metaethical internalism: Another neglected distinction. *Journal of Ethics* 13:51–72.

Wheeler, Jack. 1986. Rand and Aristotle: A comparison of Objectivist and Aristotelian ethics. In *The philosophic thought of Ayn Rand*, ed. Douglas Den Uyl and Douglas Rasmussen, 81–101. Urbana: University of Illinois Press.

Wiggins, David. A sensible subjectivism. In *Needs, values, truth: Essays in the philosophy of value*. New York: Oxford University Press.

———. 1995. Eudaimonism and realism in Aristotle's ethics: A reply to John McDowell. In Heinaman 2005, 219–31.

Williams, Bernard. 1985. *Ethics and the limits of philosophy*. Cambridge, MA: Harvard University Press.

Wilson, David Sloan. 1989. Levels of selection: An alternative to individualism in biology and the human sciences. *Social Networks* 11:257–72.

Wright, Darryl. 2005. Needs of the *psyche* in Ayn Rand's early ethical thought. In *Essays on Ayn Rand's* Anthem, ed. R. Mayhew, 149–81. Lanham, MD: Lexington Books.

———. 2008. Evaluative concepts and objective values: Rand on moral objectivity. In *Objectivism, subjectivism, and relativism in ethics*, ed. E. F. Paul, F. Miller Jr., and J. Paul, 253–74. New York: Cambridge University Press.

———. 2011. A social being. In Gotthelf and Salmieri 2011.

Young, Julian. 2006. *Nietzsche's philosophy of religion*. New York: Cambridge University Press.

Paul Bloomfield is associate professor of philosophy at the University of Connecticut, Storrs. He is the author of *Moral Reality* (2001) and the editor of *Morality and Self-Interest* (2008), in addition to a number of articles on metaethics and moral philosophy. He is currently working on a book manuscript entitled *A Theory of the Good Life*.

Helen Cullyer is associate program officer in scholarly communications and information technology at the Andrew W. Mellon Foundation. She was formerly assistant professor of classics at the University of Pittsburgh where she was director of the interdepartmental graduate program in classics, philosophy, and ancient science. Her research interests are in ancient ethics and politics, and she has published articles and book chapters on Aristotle and the Stoics. Her book on the virtue of *megalopsychia* (greatness of soul) is forthcoming from Cambridge University Press.

Allan Gotthelf is multiyear visiting professor of history and philosophy of science at the University of Pittsburgh, where he holds the University's Fellowship for the Study of Objectivism. He was one of the founding members of the Ayn Rand Society and, as its secretary, chairs its steering committee. He is the author of *On Ayn Rand* (2000) and coeditor of the forthcoming *Ayn Rand: A Companion to Her Works and Thought* (2011). He has also published extensively on Aristotle; a volume of his papers, *Teleology, First Principles, and Scientific Method in Aristotle's Biology*, is forthcoming.

Lester H. Hunt is professor of philosophy at the University of Wisconsin, Madison. He has also taught at Carnegie Mellon University and The Johns Hopkins University. He is the author of *Nietzsche and the Origins of Virtue* (1990) and *Character and Culture* (1998), and is the author of articles on ethics, political philosophy, and the presentation of ideas in literature and in film. He is currently working on a book on the political philosophy of Robert Nozick.

Irfan Khawaja is assistant professor of philosophy at Felician College (Lodi, NJ), and editor (with Carrie-Ann Biondi) of *Reason Papers: A Journal of Interdisciplinary Normative Studies*. He is the author of "Why They Hate Us: A Pedagogical Proposal," in *Philosophy of Education in the Era of Globalization* (2010) and "Religious Indoctrination and the Wish for the Irrevocable," in *Religious Upbringing and the Costs of Freedom: Personal and Philosophical Essays on the Morality of Indoctrination* (2010).

James G. Lennox is professor of history and philosophy of science at the University of Pittsburgh and one of the founding members of the Ayn Rand Society. He is author of *Aristotle's Philosophy of Biology* (2001) and *Aristotle on the Parts of Animals I–IV* (2001) and coeditor of *Philosophical Issues in Aristotle's Biology* (1987), *Self-Motion from Aristotle to Newton* (1995), and *Concepts, Theories, and Rationality in the Biological Sciences* (1995).

Tara Smith is professor of philosophy at the University of Texas at Austin, where she holds the BB&T Chair for the Study of Objectivism and is the Anthem Foundation Fellow. She is the author of *Ayn Rand's Normative Ethics: The Virtuous Egoist* (2006), *Viable Values: A Study of Life as the Root and Reward of Morality* (2000), and *Moral Rights and Political Freedom* (1995), as well as numerous articles spanning such subjects as purported rights conflicts, everyday justice, forgiveness, friendship, pride, moral perfection, the nature of objectivity, and judicial decision making. Her current research centers around objectivity in the law.

Christine Swanton has taught in the philosophy department of the University of Auckland, New Zealand, for many years, having received her B.Phil. and D.Phil. at Oxford University. She has published extensively on ethics and related topics, and especially on virtue ethics. She is the author of *Virtue Ethics: A Pluralistic View* (2003, rpt. 2005) and is currently working on the virtue ethics of Hume and Nietzsche.

Darryl Wright is professor of philosophy at Harvey Mudd College (The Claremont Colleges). He works in the areas of moral and political philosophy and has published several articles on Ayn Rand's ethical thought as well as articles on G. E. Moore and F. H. Bradley. Recent publications include "Evaluative Concepts and Objective Values: Rand on Moral Objectivity" (in *Social Philosophy and Policy*) and "Ayn Rand's Ethics: From *The Fountainhead* to *Atlas Shrugged*" (in *Essays on Ayn Rand's* Atlas Shrugged). He is currently writing a book on Ayn Rand's ethics in relation to contemporary (meta)ethical theories.